MUD LAKE

By Sam Lovall

in collaboration with

Bridget Booth, Chris Earley, Becky Goodman, Beth Hagenbuch,
Susan Lovall, Mark Nimphie, and Terry Sack

ENVIRONMENTAL LAW INSTITUTE
Washington, D.C.

1730 M Street NW, Washington, DC 20036

Published February 2024.

Printed in the United States of America
ISBN 978-1-58576-267-5

Table of Contents

Meet the Authors

Sam Lovall (lead author and illustrator) has over 35 years of professional landscape architectural experience in design, construction, and grant writing for park, riverfront, trail, urban, and environmental planning projects, in addition to teaching Landscape Architecture classes at Michigan State University. He served as Project Manager for numerous riparian planning projects in southeast Michigan, including the development of master plans for the Rouge River Gateway, the Detroit River International Wildlife Refuge Gateway Site, and multiple habitat restoration projects in the Lower Detroit River. In 2020, Sam received the Environmental Law Institute's National Wetlands Award for Local Stewardship. Sam has always found Mud Lake to be a special place for enjoyment with family, close friends, or alone. Every visit was unique based on seasonal changes and slowly evolving environmental conditions. This interest in the natural world is what lured him into the study of landscape architecture.

Bridget Booth is an eighth-grade science teacher at Haslett Middle School and a certified environmental educator in Michigan. She got her start at Woldumar Nature Center in Lansing, Michigan, and has been taking students outdoors to learn ever since. She is past president and board member of the Michigan Alliance for Environmental and Outdoor Education and now leads their Climate Education Action Team. Bridget, her husband, and two sons spend spare time reading, playing in the woods, and exploring places like Mud Lake and the Great Lakes.

Chris Earley (Cricket) is a retired social worker for the state of Michigan. Chris provided a public service to mostly underprivileged citizens of Michigan for more than 40 years, rooted in an understanding of how large-scale natural processes are greater than us and can impact our lives. Of his four children and 11 grandchildren, several continue exploring and fishing at Mud Lake.

Becky Goodman served as Downtown Director for the City of Petoskey, Michigan, for the past 19 years, previously having directed downtown activities for the city of Lake Orion, Michigan, for another five years. Mud Lake was where her brother would go for long periods of time and not be around to tease or taunt her and her friends. While collaborating on this book, the importance of Mud Lake resonated. The swampiness, the bugs, the snakes, and even the mud subliminally led her to a career in downtown development–a meaningful part of the circle.

Beth Hagenbuch is a landscape architect who was raised on the edge of Mud Lake's surrounding marsh where some of the mud stuck, fostering a lifelong interest in the environment, ecology, and our place in it. After living in a variety of incredible environments including the Rocky Mountains, the Yucatan peninsula, Texas, Florida, Great Britain, and California, she now lives in Farmington Hills, Michigan, where her work allows her to focus on sustainable landscapes, local food systems, and urban design.

Susan Lovall, Grandmother and Mud Lake Enthusiast, grew up on a farm six miles from Haslett, Michigan. Her parents' best friends farmed the property near Mud Lake, but it wasn't until her acquaintance with Brent that she became fully engaged with the lake. Their relationship revolved around an appreciation for natural landscapes, consuming their free time as young adults. Susan is responsible for passing that passion on to their three children and seven grandchildren and conceiving the idea for the book *Mud Lake*.

Mark Nimphie is a retired mechanical and electrical engineer. After Mark's involvement with design and engineering management for General Motors, followed by Ford Motor Company as Product Planning Director, he owned and operated a restaurant in Mackinaw City, Michigan. Early training for his accomplished career as a youngster, at primarily his mom's expense, included fun in water and mud near a swampland that was visible from his home's living room—that being Mud Lake.

Terry Sack worked in sales for the medical industry before enrolling in nursing school at age 48 to further his passion for human wellbeing. He also provides security, promotions, and support to nationally touring musical acts. Serving as a volunteer fireman, umpire, and special education substitute teacher are part of what came out of his engagement with the marshlands surrounding Mud Lake and Lake Lansing in the greater Haslett area.

Prologue

About 11,000 years ago, a deep freeze hovered over North America, lasting for centuries. A one-mile-thick ice sheet sluggishly slid over the landscape, redefining the topography. It was the last continental glacier making a slow departure. As gigantic blocks of ice broke away from the retreating ice pack, they often became buried in sediment. And as they melted, the depressions became water features, geologically known as "kettle lakes" or glacial lakes. Depressions not filled with water are known as "potholes"—the namesake for craters found in our roads every spring. Although nothing to do with glaciers, they also result from ice in the northern United States.

As the glacier crept northward, the land revegetated. Various plants supporting a wide spectrum of insects and wildlife embraced the new water bodies. Eons of seasonal growth, dieback, and decay enriched surrounding soils with organic matter, further enhancing the plant and animal environment. The process began slowly, but with every brief millennium, life on land and in water became more diverse and plentiful.

One of these glacial lakes in central Lower Michigan sits near the community of Haslett, south of the town's residential area. It's not a big lake, only a little over five acres. Known as "Mud Lake" until acquired by Haslett Public Schools along with surrounding land to construct a new high school, it was cleverly renamed Wildlife Lake. Unlike its larger counterpart to the north, Lake Lansing, Mud Lake offers little related to typical recreational activities. There are no sandy beaches, no public boat access, no nearby bars or restaurants, and it never had an amusement park with a towering roller coaster ride on its shore.

Mud Lake is exactly as its name implies. With only a few areas deeper than eight feet, its murky, black bottom is hardly visible. Shallow edges are mostly covered by lily pads, and the surrounding beach is a wet marsh that pretty much precludes foot traffic except by young kids experienced in stepping over soft, soupy terrain covered by waist-high plant growth concealing sinkholes and snakes. This marshy perimeter is expansive, stretching more than 1,500 feet on the lake's east side to Cornell Road before continuing further on the road's opposite side. Likewise, this sea of wetland extends south and beyond Tihart Road. The marsh is much narrower to the west,

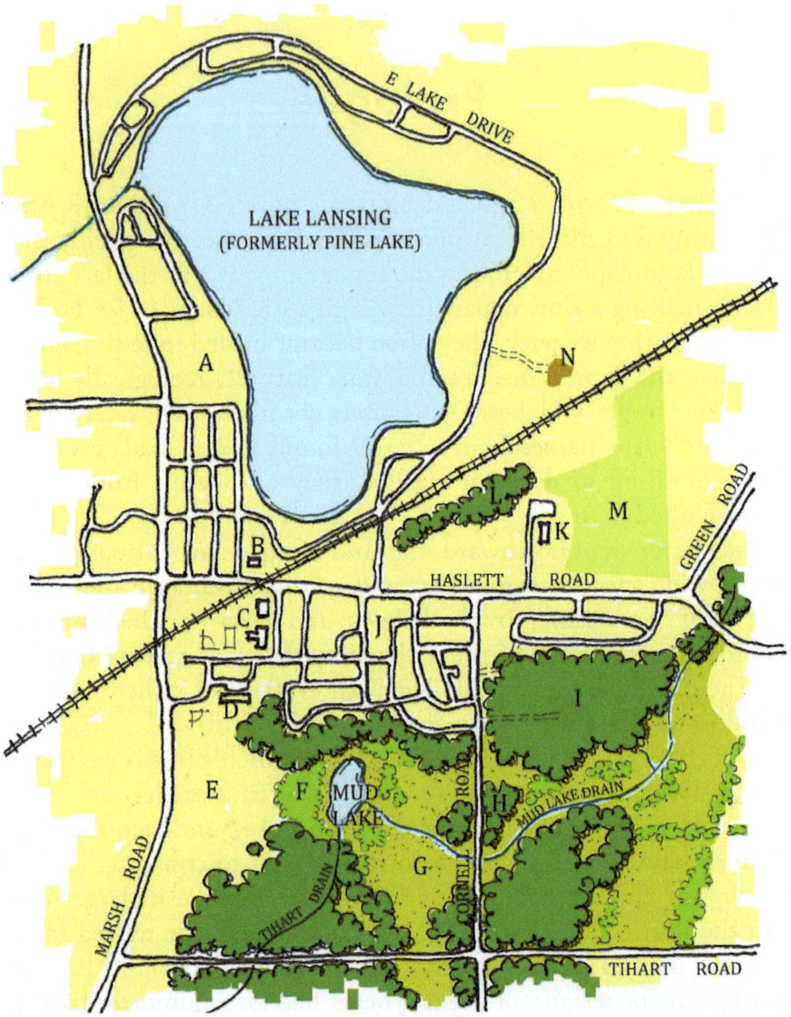

LEGEND

A LAKE LANSING AMUSEMENT PARK (Formerly Haslett Park)
B POST OFFICE (Formerly the Train Station Site)
C JUNIOR HIGH SCHOOL AND VERA RALYA ELEMENTARY SCHOOL
D HIGH SCHOOL (Later to become the Middle School)
E O'BRYANT FARM (Later to become the High School site)
F SCRUB SHRUB
G MARSH
H SAND HILLS
I THE WOODS
J LAKEVIEW HEIGHTS SUBDIVISION
K WILKSHIRE ELEMENTARY SCHOOL
L THE PINES
M PINE LAKE COUNTRY CLUB
N THE DUMP

0 1,000 500 2,000 NORTH

SCALE IN FEET

Greater Mud Lake Area
circa early 1960s

Figure 0.1. Map of the Greater Mud Lake Area

although still formidable. Here, it transitions to a scrub shrub area before reaching the new high school development that replaced farmland in the early 1970s. To the north, the marsh is equally narrow, ending at the foot of a wooded slope descending from a little-brick-house residential area.

This book conveys the importance of wetlands like the one surrounding Mud Lake, which are now known to provide valuable ecosystem services. With emerging evidence surfacing about earth heading into another period of mass extinction based on the consequences of climate change, there is consensus among scientists calling for immediate actions to halt and reverse human transformation and degradation of natural ecosystems. This means large swaths of wetlands, forests, and other natural areas must be set aside to help mitigate climate change and provide habitat for wildlife to thrive.

In 2019, the United Nations Environment Programme released a report on biodiversity indicating one million species already face extinction—many within decades. Their 2021 report echoes this concern and outlines a scientific blueprint to tackle climate, biodiversity, and pollution emergencies as part of a worldwide cultural change to make peace with nature. Wetlands are identified as the most degraded ecosystem type, making them one of the largest challenges to rethink. Fortunately, Mud Lake and its surrounding wetland survived a 200-year period of natural area destruction based on gradual but extensive land transformations initiated in the United States by European settlers. A brief historical account of how this happened in the greater Mud Lake area is presented here.

Prior to the mid-1800s, Mud Lake saw almost no human activity. It simply accepted water flowing overland from the east and emptied to the south, eventually finding the Red Cedar River on its way to the Grand River and Lake Michigan. With its rich surroundings of wetland plants, it offered incredible habitat for fish and wildlife including wolves and bears. Early human activity in this area congregated around the neighboring, larger lake, known by newcoming Europeans as Pine Lake. Native Americans, most recently including the Chippewa, resided here for thousands of years, making use of its abundant fishery, nearby fertile soils for crops, and forests for wild game. The area was a hub for trails heading in several directions toward other places near lakes and rivers offering similar life-sustaining resources.

In 1836, Obed Marshall was the first settler to purchase property near Mud Lake in the newly established township of Meridian, eventually to contain the unincorporated communities of Okemos and Haslett. He acquired nearly 500 acres for a sum of $318.08 from the U.S. Land Office.

It included 160 acres between Pine and Mud Lakes, the nucleus of what later became Haslett. Other settlers followed, seeking inexpensive land and homes in the wilderness. While farms sprung up on high ground, the community center remained near the south end of Pine Lake.

The Pine Lake Hotel, constructed on the lake's north shore in the 1870s, featured a dance hall, a bathhouse, boathouses, and an icehouse, along with swings and other waterfront amenities under a cooling tree canopy. A small steamer was launched in 1876, hosting rides for 150 people and providing transportation to the hotel from the lake's south end. Excellent boating and fishing opportunities attracted up to 6,000 people on the best summer days. The railroad came through the area in 1879/1880, fueling even more popularity for the lake as a recreational site. After completing the inner-urban trolley from Lansing to Pine Lake, the area quickly transitioned into a trendy summer destination.

In the late 1800s, a group known as the Michigan Spiritualists began holding meetings on the lake's southwest shore. As attendance grew heavy, a flurry of land swapping occurred until James H. Haslett, a haberdasher from Port Huron, acquired most of the land for these gatherings. Later to become known as Haslett Park, the 20-acre parcel showcased a beautiful grove of oak, hickory, and elm trees, greatly enhancing the charm of this lakeshore site. Objectives for the park sought by Mr. Haslett included:

1. Offer an attractive resort for all disciples, professors, or inquirers about Spiritualism and related philosophically and religiously considered materials or manifestations.

2. Teach Spiritualism—discuss truth and freedom against error and superstition.

3. Provide a beautiful spot for outdoor meetings—also for those seeking pleasure only.

4. Establish a home for aged people and orphans.

5. Establish a sanitarium.

6. Develop an art gallery—include work by spirit hands.

Haslett Park became the meeting place for the "Haslett Park Club Circle," an 1890 support group for the Spiritualist camp. In promoting camp meetings and events, the club aspired for Haslett Park to become America's mecca for Spiritualists—a vision that would attract followers from around the entire country. But it never happened. The dream fizzled in 1891 when

James Haslett passed away. With his leadership gone, most attendees soon refocused elsewhere.

The 60-by-96-foot, open-sided meeting pavilion, constructed of heavy timbers, was repurposed in 1934 as the "Dodgem," a wild bumper car ride, when the grounds became an exciting amusement park. The Pine Lake Hotel burned down in 1929 but was replaced by the Dells Ballroom where many big-name bands of the day performed. This continued into the 1960s, featuring names like Bill Haley and His Comets, Chuck Berry, and Rare Earth, while Lake Lansing Amusement Park thrived as the main attraction for over 40 years. Amusements included a state-of-the-art, wooden roller coaster, an ornate carousel, pony rides, a Ferris wheel, a mini-railroad, concession stands, arcade games, high-twirling airplanes, a Tilt-A-Whirl, dodgem cars, picnic grounds, and more.

By the early 1900s, Pine Lake was ringed with seasonal cottages and became a vital destination for summertime fun. The amusement park and dance hall attracted folks from nearby cities by offering a needed reprieve, particularly in the Great Depression years. During this time, another offshore nightclub supported by wood piers, accessible only by boat, doubled as a speakeasy. Known as the "Izzer Club," it was equipped with a trapdoor for disposing booze if lawmen were seen to be approaching. Throughout all this mayhem, Mud Lake continued providing ecosystem services for birds, insects, fish, turtles, frogs, and snakes. Although having few human visitors, its life-support rating registered extremely high.

Following World War II, a housing boom for homecoming servicemembers and their families swept over the county, and Haslett was no exception. In the early 1950s, several new subdivisions appeared. Lakeview Heights was sandwiched between Mud Lake and Haslett Road, the main drag through town, and Wilkshire popped up a few years later not far to the east. Hillbrook Park came during this same time a little west of town.

With new homes numbering in the thousands, you could not travel in any neighborhood without seeing kids everywhere on bikes, playing games, socializing in groups, or just wandering about. They organized their own sports and play without parental involvement or supervision. The schools were bursting at the seams, and classrooms could not be built fast enough. Two new Haslett elementary schools were needed to accommodate the crowd.

Many fathers were veterans of World War II or Korea, and for the most part, mothers were homemakers. For young boys, play often mimicked recent wars. Playing "army" could mean fighting Nazis or choosing sides to reenact the Battle of Gettysburg, reflecting the ongoing Civil War Centennial recognition. And don't forget the Alamo! Davy Crockett was a hero among seven-year-olds flaunting jackknives and coonskin caps. Diverse places of employment for Haslett folks ranged from factory work at Oldsmobile or Motor Wheel, to making use of Ph.D.s at Michigan State University, with all sorts of businessmen, doctors, and lawyers in the mix.

How Mud Lake and its natural surroundings impacted the lives of these young families carries a repetitive theme. Short adventure stories expressing shared, underlying messages fill this book's early chapters, characterized by youngsters experiencing the natural world during the 1950s, '60s, and early '70s. The stories illustrate how natural spaces enriched spirits and served as learning laboratories. The unfolding of historical events during the 1960s are summarized, giving context to how people perceived the natural world and how they prioritized environmental quality during these times. The concept of circular energy is identified and found worthy of further investigation. This cosmic energy field fueling the movement of celestial bodies, glaciers, water, carbon, and life itself is examined and provides a basis for big-picture explanations. After the kids in adventure land advance their mobility modes from bicycles to automobiles, a glitch in the carbon cycle becomes apparent that upsets the forecast for everyone's future. As our atmosphere becomes overloaded with carbon emissions, it is clear that earth is embarking on a climate change. Circular movements associated with climate change are presented along with strategies for mitigation and adaptation. Mud Lake and its surrounding natural area stand out as guiding examples for future restoration work based on their long history of sustaining wildlife and profound effect on human lives.

References

Telephone Interviews and E-mail Correspondence With Bridget Booth, Certified Environmental Educator, Science Teacher at Haslett Middle School (Mar. 2 - Apr. 22, 2022).

Telephone Interviews and E-mail Correspondence With Chris Earley, Retired Social Worker for the state of Michigan (Mar. 10 - Apr. 14, 2022).

Conversations With Susan Lovall, Grandmother and Mud Lake Enthusiast (Nov. 2021 - Dec. 2022).

National Aeronautics and Space Administration (NASA) Global Climate Change, *Scientific Consensus: Earth's Climate Is Warming*, https://climate.nasa.gov/scientific-consensus/ (last visited May 31, 2023).

Evelyn Huber Raphael, A History of the Haslett-Lake Lansing Area, Meridian Township, Ingham County, Michigan (1958, revised 1974) (distributed by the Haslett Women's Club).

John Robinson, *Haslett, Michigan, Had A Spiritualist Camp at Lake Lansing From 1882-1890s,* 99.1 WFMK (Oct. 6, 2021), 99wfmk.com/lake-lansing-spiritualist-camp/.

United Nations Environment Programme, Making Peace With Nature: A Scientific Blueprint to Tackle the Climate, Biodiversity, and Pollution Emergencies (2021), https://wedocs.unep.org/xmlui/bitstream/handle/20.500.11822/34948/MPN.pdf.

World Is "on Notice" as Major UN Report Shows One Million Species Face Extinction, United Nations News (May 6, 2019), https://news.un.org/en/story/2019/05/1037941.

Chapter 1
Mud Lake Surroundings

For the youngsters of Lakeview Heights, Mud Lake was enticing partly because it was so hard to get there. Although not a long hike, it became treacherous when getting close. The surrounding marsh was a wet one. One wrong step and you could be up to your waist in muck. A popular access route, which minimized the marsh-crossing distance, required making a dash through private property on Biscayne Way, near its west end. After passing between the houses, it was a search for a remnant of the previous summer's path through a thick and wet woodland. The path was usually overgrown due to little use, but after a brief battle with opposing undergrowth, it opened to a scrub shrub area northwest of the lake. From here, it was whatever way looked best to approach the lake's west shore, where the marsh ring appeared to be at its narrowest. In this last leg to the water, one could count on getting wet feet at a minimum. And upon arrival, there was still no stable edge to support standing on dry ground.

Since an expedition to the lake was not possible without a muddy, wet return, 10- and 11-year-old boys often chose alternate routes not involving a potential confrontation with property owners on Biscayne Way. A couple of these routes required hiking or biking to make use of either Mud Lake Drain (known as First Creek) or Tihart Drain, sometimes called Second Creek or Tihart Creek, where these waterways intersected Cornell and Tihart Roads. Some kids would argue that the real Second Creek was further south on Cornell Road, but no one knew where. This ambiguity often caused some confusion when reporting wilderness excursions to the neighborhood gang. Regardless, both access options involved wading down one of the creeks through the extensive marsh area to reach the lake. This was a slow go, but eventful along the way, and there was a slim chance of becoming lost, which could happen if one strayed from the creek out into the marsh.

The abundance of turtles and frogs in either creek presented a catching contest with every several steps, slowing down the trip, sometimes to the point of having to turn back without ever reaching the lake due to time constraints. If time was known to be short, a simple trip to First Creek could be adequate. The gigantic, corrugated metal pipe that conveyed the creek under

Cornell road was exposed on both ends. The top of the pipe offered warm and dry surfaces to lie flat on one's belly with head extended over the edge, upside down, to investigate any action happening in the pipe under the road. And if getting wet feet was needed, it could be accomplished in minutes on either side of the road with no shortage of frogs and turtles to catch.

An obscure patch of high ground screened by roadside trees laid a little north of First Creek on the east side of Cornell Road. Explorations found this area to be mostly sand, which led to its naming: "Sand Hills." This undulating, sandy landform surrounded by swamp seemed out of place, but no one asked questions that would reveal having visited the site to avoid any accusation of trespassing, even though the "no trespassing" signs posted along the roadside were not regarded as applicable to kids. What's more peculiar than this out-of-place sand pile was a circular pond, not more than 50 feet across, at the Sand Hills north end that offered a cooling dip on hot summer days. However, caution was heeded when approaching the pond due to an extensive patch of stinging nettles. One bare-skinned brush with these plants would imbed an image of their identity for life into the minds of young explorers, coupled with a temporary burning rash.

A little further north, a fun-filled woodlot known as "the Woods" occupied high ground on this same side of Cornell Road. It had two visibly different zones divided by a woven wire fence running north and south, containing cows that occasionally grazed in the easterly area. The westerly section was easily accessed by a two-track lane stemming from Cornell Road. Not far down the lane, an abandoned car spoiled the area's natural beauty but offered something to investigate and a target for carriers of .22 caliber rifles. It eventually took on the look of Bonnie and Clyde's last getaway car—when they didn't get away. Adding to the excitement, hikers could almost count on confronting a garter snake or two, or more, sunbathing on the lane.

The two-track trail eventually deteriorated into a footpath leading to a hole in the wire fence large enough for small bodies to pass. Once on the other side, everything changed. The trees were larger with a tighter canopy, and the temperature was noticeably cooler. The ground, although well-covered with woodland forbs, did not impede foot traffic due to sporadic cropping by cows. To newcomers, an eerie spookiness set in after the fence crossing due to the darker surroundings that became notably wilder. A low-swooping owl could appear out of nowhere, disrupting the stillness when least expected, raising any visitor's adrenaline.

The main attraction near the Woods' far back edge originated when the property owner dumped a sizable pile of stumps and logs against a large maple

Figure 1.1. Map of immediate area surrounding Mud Lake

tree. Over time, smaller branches fell onto the pile, filling voids between the top logs enough to catch fallen leaves. These eventually decayed to a compost supporting herbaceous growth. The exciting part was found below the green roof, where passageways and spaces randomly connected when the tree parts were originally placed. The kids discovered a small opening at ground level to access this maze of dark tunnels and rooms. One space was large enough to contain three or four kids, and with the help of flashlights, offered a meeting place to discuss whatever activity might be next. The decaying timber's texture and reddish-ocher coloration together with its damp musty scent created a unique interior ambiance. This was unquestionably a special place within the Woods known as the Fox Den.

The trees in the front section of the Woods were less mature than those in the back with a few exceptions. A spectacular beech tree grew well north of the lane, with no defined pathway to its location. Only experienced woods-kids could find it. Known for incredible climbing, the tree's smooth gray bark offered endless opportunities for carving autographs or someone-plus-someone notations. From a lookout perch near the top, the tip of the state capitol dome in downtown Lansing, over eight miles away, emerged above the distant tree canopy line.

Another great climbing tree thrived closer to Cornell Road, near another two-track lane connecting the Lakeview Heights and Wilkshire subdivisions. This was an unusually massive American elm having main branches larger in diameter than most mature tree trunks. Most of these branches grew out of the tree's central stem true to form, in a fountain-like manner, while others extended horizontally through the interior of the tree's canopy, crisscrossing in multiple locations. The result was a tangle of large, live timber, a little like the Fox Den, where passageways and spaces made an enchanting play place. Yet it was all high above ground and well-ventilated with views to the surroundings. It was a tree house of sorts, without any added boards from a lumberyard—except for several planks nailed to the trunk, giving aid to short climbers in getting to the tree's lowest branches.

Figure 1.2. Giant American elm tree.

A smaller woodlot provided a second outdoor adventure anchor on the west side of Lakeview Heights, bordering on Mud Lake's scrub shrub and marsh area. Being adjacent to homes along Biscayne Way and Woodville Road, it provided amazing opportunities for youngsters to experience the natural world right in their own backyards. Cutting through this woods from the neighborhood to the schools immersed kids in nature every day, whether they wanted it or not. Steep downward slopes to the south and west enhanced woodland romping opportunities. Although identified by the same name as the Woods east of Cornell Road, there was rarely any confusion about which woods was the topic of conversation. If needed, it was easily clarified.

In the Woods (this one—the one near the schools—not the one by Cornell Road), two ponds offered year-round fun. The smaller one nudged against neighborhood property lines, giving easy access to pollywog dipping, and the larger one laid on the west edge of the Woods at the base of a hill. Both ponds received frequent visits from nearby kids causing regular clothes changes. In winter, the larger one served as a slippery landing for sledders, extending the ride for kids—and adults who couldn't resist reliving a bumpy, downhill slide with a face full of snow.

A historic log cabin occupied a high point near the middle of the Woods. Constructed around 1970 with help from school kids, it served as a teaching tool for Outdoor Education and Log Cabin Living classes. Although eventually relocated to the "Historic Village" at the township hall, the Woods' adventure value remained intact.

References

Telephone Interviews and E-mail Correspondence With Beth Hagenbuch, Landscape Architect (Feb. 11 - Apr. 5, 2022).

Telephone Interviews and E-mail Correspondence With Chris Earley, Retired Social Worker for the state of Michigan (Mar. 10 - Apr. 14, 2022).

Telephone Interviews and E-mail Correspondence With Mark Nimphie, Retired Mechanical/Electrical Engineer (Mar. 5 - Apr. 14, 2022).

Conversations With Susan Lovall, Grandmother and Mud Lake Enthusiast (Nov. 2021 - Dec. 2022).

Chapter 2
First Visit to Mud Lake

Mud Lake and its surrounding natural features offered exciting adventures for kids in the new housing developments. These new homes, although small with only a few floor plan choices, were constructed of substantial materials—brick exteriors, wood floors, and plastered walls—and most had full basements, which eventually became needed additional bedroom space. They were attractive to first-time home buyers with young families, resulting in an immediate increase in Haslett's youth population. The new neighborhood, with comfortably sized lots and almost no fences, together with the surrounding natural area, provided ideal open space for youngsters to explore and socialize.

The Lovall family was among the first residents to find a home on Buckingham Road. With two children, Becky and Brent, they exposed their son to the wonders of Mud Lake before he was of age to make the trip on his own. Brent's father, Sam, had fond memories of his childhood ice fishing excursions in a rural area on Michigan's west side, prompting a medley of fishing-related Christmas presents for Brent when he was just nine years old. These included a hole-cutting spud that he could barely pick up, an ice skimmer, a Coleman lantern, two fiberglass fishing poles, two tip-ups, a minnow bucket, and an assortment of hooks, bobbers, and sinkers. Due to the odd shapes, nothing was giftwrapped other than the spoon part of the ice skimmer. However, the skimmer's handle end and spud had bows, and the hooks, bobbers, and sinkers were tucked into a stocking. The fishing poles simply leaned against the wall in a corner next to the tree, but when the tree lights were turned on, they were immediate eye grabbers.

Conversely, Becky's main gift was neatly wrapped. When opened, it looked like an odd suitcase. Becky proceeded to undo the latches and pull up the top. From the look on her face when the camera flashed, this was apparently something she really wanted—a clarinet! Brent did not quite understand what all the hoopla was about and had no clue what to do with his new stuff, but the idea of walking out onto an ice-covered lake to catch fish sounded great.

With the ice on Mud Lake being too thin, the wait seemed like forever. Finally, on New Year's Day, a whole week later, Sam drives by Lake Lansing, looking for people on the ice. Seeing flocks of them all over the lake, he determines it's time to go. No wind and enough sunshine to hold the temperature slightly above freezing made it perfect. So, they pack their gear into the Ford Falcon and proceed to O'Bryant's farm where Sam asks permission to access Mud Lake. From here, it was a short walk through a snow-covered field and the scrub shrub area to the marsh ring surrounding the lake. Being frozen, it posed no mud problem.

Brent's first steps onto the ice were made with hesitation, as the edge was quite thin and could potentially break. Once past the edge, it seemed plenty safe, and its slipperiness begged for some running and sliding before getting into the serious business of fishing. A little vigorous activity warmed Brent's bones, while Sam did the same by spudding two holes through the ice. Before too long, a loud groaning sound seemed to come from under the water and move across the lake. What was that?! Sam let Brent know it was just the ice cracking, which squelched the running and sliding and cued up the fishing.

Not much happened right off the bat other than some nibbles that required impaling more corn borers onto the specially crafted "teardrop" hooks. They were equipped with tiny metal shields, each painted differently—white with a red dot, black with a yellow dot, neon green with an orange dot, and so on. How could a fish pass these up? BB-sized, split shot, lead sinkers were pinched onto the fishline several inches above the hook. Oval-shaped cork bobbers held their position on the line at the water's surface with brightly red-painted, slender wood dowels penetrating a central hole in the cork. Sam instructed Brent to occasionally raise and lower the bobber. This is called "jigging." He should do this repetitively in short, quick motions and sporadically interject a higher, slow pull, for variety, to attract fish. This technique is similar to jigging in summer conditions, except that when ice fishing, it should be done a bit harder and more erratically. In addition, since fish will rarely strike a fast-moving lure in winter, periods of jigging should slow to a stop, allowing some time for fish to strike. Most strikes occur when bait movement slows down or right after it stops.

After an hour or so of bouncing fish bait up and down eight to 20 inches off the lake bottom with no significant action, Sam determines that new holes would likely yield success, or maybe he just needed to warm up. Regardless, he spuds two fresh holes about 50 feet away. As the sun drops lower in the sky, the temperature heads in the same direction. This dip below freezing introduces new problems. Splashes from the jigging process cause ice to build up on the line above the bobber, which has to be removed by chewing—most effectively with gloves off. And the ice skimmer has to be kept handy for frequent hole maintenance.

With the temperature dropping further as twilight advanced, fingers and toes began to get numb, and the red-painted wood dowels in the bobbers did not look very bright. Just when wondering if he had the wrong-colored hook, Brent's bobber darts downward out of sight. Not knowing exactly what to do, he instinctively pulls his pole up. With that, the tip of his rod did some wild bending, which obviously meant something was going on down there. Sam tells Brent to just back away from the hole. When he does, out pops a fat yellow perch. Wow, now this was exciting! Before Sam could assist Brent, his bobber sinks, and up comes a good-sized bluegill. Gloves come off to dehook the fish and to do some bait maintenance—then back in the holes. Immediately, both bobbers sink again, and two more fish appear on the ice. This action keeps going for a half hour or so—long enough to fill the bucket before slowing down. By then it was dark, and four hands were frozen from no chance to put on gloves. So, after gathering their gear, as night was closing in, they hiked back through the brush to the car. Warming up was a slow process that wasn't complete until well after arriving home. But it was worth it. What a blast!

References

Conversations and E-mail Correspondence With Becky Goodman, Downtown Director, City of Petoskey (Feb. 22 - Apr. 28, 2022).

Chapter 3
The Big Catch

Ice fishing trips to Mud Lake became the favorite weekend activity for Sam and Brent that year and for several winters to follow. Not every trip produced a full bucket of fish, but all offered something to make the next trip a welcome event. Although the lake was never crowded, Sam and Brent were often joined by other fishermen. Two regulars placed a wooden shanty near the lake's south end. What a great idea. Stepping inside was a treat. No wind and heat generated by a Coleman lantern completely changed the atmosphere, and two small windows allowed views outside. Furnishings included two folding chairs straddling a small table with half-full beers and a transistor radio tuned into the Spartan basketball game, live from Jenison Fieldhouse in East Lansing.

Besides enjoying a non-workday, the goal here was to catch a northern pike or two. Inside the shanty, a rectangular hole through the ice was much larger than any outside, making the place borderline dangerous for kids. Sliced potatoes covered the lake bottom beneath the hole to lighten its appearance and provide a contrasting background for any dark-colored dorsal fish skin passing through the area. Two fish decoys resembling small perch dangled about a foot above the potatoes, and the men were equipped with long, seven-tined spears. They would take turns making a stab with each passing pike. When one appeared, it came in slowly, showing curiosity about the non-skittish perch decoys. The spear was then gently dipped into the water without a ripple and plunged into the pike, just behind its head. This seemed like a great way to catch fish, but Brent could not convince his dad.

Sam preferred using tip-ups with live bait (large minnows) that could be placed in a couple locations on the lake and easily moved if not productive. In addition, Sam's fishing outfit did not require the comfort of a shanty. Acquired during his U.S. Navy days, his blackish-green bib overalls were a heavy material that could hardly bend—possibly suitable for a moonwalk. And the gray hooded sweatshirt from the same source was almost too heavy for Brent to lift. His leather mittens with removable wool lining were only brought along for emergencies. Sam seldom wore them due to all the bait maintenance, fish dehooking, and Lucky Strike cigarette lighting.

Tip-ups are ingenious contraptions made of wood members that unfold from a middle joint into a cross-shaped object. A reel of fishing line is attached to the end of one of the cross members. The reel gets slightly unwound, and the line is equipped with a hook, sinker, and minnow. When ready to go, the reel and baited line are placed through a hole in the ice, while the other cross member sits horizontally on the ice surface to keep the device from falling through the hole. A narrow steel ribbon with a small red flag is attached to the top end of the vertical cross member. When setting the tip-up, the flag is pulled down and clipped to the reel, putting tension on the steel ribbon to spring back to its upright position. Any movement of the reel, like what happens when a fish strikes, releases the clip, and the flag pops up. So, one can be jigging for bluegills and have a chance to catch a northern pike at the same time.

Sam always liked to set the tip-ups near the lake's inlet, First Creek, thinking a little moving water might be a natural attraction for pike. Jigging was done along a shallow drop off on the lake's opposite side. Rushing to investigate popped-up flags typically resulted in false alarms due to gusting wind but served as a temporary body warmer.

Finally, the day comes when jogging across the lake ends with something on the line. Sam pulls the tip-up from the hole and gives the line a jerk to set the hook, then proceeds to pull in the line. With this agitation, whatever was down there decides to make a run for it. So, Sam lets him go with a little resistance to wear him down. When the fish appears to surrender, Sam resumes pulling in the line, while Brent winds it back onto the reel. Just as this monster fish shows his face coming through the hole, he throws the hook and retreats downward. Uh-oh! Sam decides it's not over and, lying flat on the ice, extends his arm through the hole up to his shoulder. Within seconds, he pulls back out of the icy water with his fingers inserted in the pike's gill.

After letting go, it flopped around on the ice a bit showing off its size—noticeably larger than any seen speared in the shanty. Brent had no idea fish came that big. Sam decided a smoke break with a Lucky was in order while Brent gathered the gear. Although this trip ended abruptly, its excitement was like no other.

Chapter 4
A Summer Visit to Mud Lake

Knowing Mud Lake to be a great fishing place, a summertime trip seemed fitting to Brent. However, Sam had no interest in wallowing through the marsh only to reach the water with no boat or any practical way to shore fish. He adamantly refused the idea, and for Brent's welfare, he declared the lake "off limits," not allowing Brent to visit the lake on his own. This decision was supported by Brent's mother, Marilyn, and made known to Becky, who watched over Brent when their parents were away. That happened every day after school since both parents worked outside the home.

Sam's ruling didn't sit well with Brent, particularly after becoming friends with L.J. Getzen, who was three years older and undoubtedly the most skilled critter catcher in the area. He had pens in his backyard for keeping captured creatures—turtles, snakes, rabbits, pigeons, and more. And he was highly experienced in travels to Mud Lake, always coming home with a live souvenir. Before long, L.J. convinced Brent that a fishing trip to the lake would be plenty safe, providing they followed First Creek to get there. It was late spring, and school was still in session. So, the trip had to be squeezed into a few hours before both kids were expected home for dinner. Becky did not need to know about the plan and was glad to get Brent out of her hair at any opportunity, especially after the two had been cooped up in the house together over the winter.

They rode their bikes down Cornell Road to minimize travel time and quickly ditched them out of sight when they arrived at First Creek. Once into the creek, frogs and turtles scrambled to safety from their sunbathing positions, and as the two youngsters splashed down the drainage way, herpetofauna continued to disappear in front of them. Both Blanding's and painted turtles seemed to be everywhere. The Blanding's, which are less common, were more desirable to catch. Given their more friendly nature, they would rarely bite. But they were all passed over that day, as this was a trip to catch fish.

The journey to the lake was anything but quiet. Bullfrogs bellowed for their mates from both sides of the creek, while bees buzzed around spring blooms, and deer flies circled the boys' heads. Splashes from who knows what, set off by the boys' chatter, randomly sounded up ahead. Red-winged blackbirds joined the commotion, noticeable by their distinctive appearance and constant scolding for invading their territory. However, the startling sound of a great blue heron taking flight sent the most alarming message, informing the boys they were unwelcome visitors.

When reaching the lakeshore, a brief exploration was undertaken to find a stable place for standing with not much luck. So, they made the best of it by trying to stay on top of grassy sedge mounds. Both boys came equipped with cane poles. Brent's pole was transported in five sections that required quick assembly, while L.J.'s pole arrived in one 10-foot-long piece. Wasting no time, using crawler-baited hooks, the fishing commenced with disappointment. The maximum distance for tossing their bait did not reach water of any depth. Bobber adjustment was necessary. Fixing the bobbers at only 18 inches above the hook allowed them to float in an upright position instead of flat on the water. But would there be any fish in this shallow water depth? Yes! Action starts immediately. Unfortunately, their bobbers only slide horizontally and never truly sink. After a brief time, this activity slows down and finally stops. Bait checks find they were robbed by little guys having no chance of swallowing the hook. So, L.J. decides to wade out into the lake in search of deeper water. Finding it a slow go as his feet sink into the muck, he lobs his bobber as far as possible, off to the right a bit, near a mass of lily pads. Before the bobber could set itself, a huge fish breaks the water surface taking his hook and reenters with a splash. L.J. yanks the pole back, and out comes the fish flying toward shore. It lands behind the boys between some red-twigged dogwoods, partly covered by water. After some flip-flopping and splashing about, tangling the line in the shrubbery, L.J. gets his hands on the fish and identifies it as the largest bass he had ever seen. With his line in a hopeless mess and the hook lodged deeply in the bass' throat, he cuts the line away from the hook

Figure 4.1. L.J.'s bass flying overhead into the brush.

and pole, allowing the fish and pole to be pulled from the thicket. That was it—L.J. was done. He puts the fish in his bucket and states, "It's time to go!"

The trip back was quick. With no time to linger, they sloshed their way back upstream not noticing anything more to catch. L.J. was thinking about how his mother would make his fish into a great dinner. She was very tolerant of him bringing home wild game and would often turn his catch into a meal. Brent sampled fried frog legs as a guest at L.J.'s home, and he found them to be quite tasty.

Brent reached his house in time to hose down in the backyard before his parents arrived. Becky was seated on the living room floor, focused on a game of double solitaire with her next-door friend, Diane. Cards laid neatly organized in long columns in front of them indicated this game had been going for quite some time. What an opportunity for Brent's tornado hands to spoil the moment, but he subdued the urge. The girls were delighted to not have Brent pestering that afternoon. So, no questions were asked about his absence, but his mind's image of the bass flying overhead was hard to not mention.

Chapter 5
Fishing With Friends

Fishing on Mud Lake became a regular thing for Brent over the next decade. Although after learning the impracticality of summer excursions, winter became the preferred time to go. Weekly trips were common. Two trips in one weekend could happen if the weather was good—or even three times, which occurred one Sunday, following a Saturday outing, when Sam forgot to bring their bait. Brent did a quick hike home and back to retrieve the wax worms, marking his third trip.

To Brent's surprise when returning, Sam already had fish flopping around him. With no other anglers in sight, where could he have gotten any bait? Sam explained how the patches of golden rod in the scrub shrub area are full of little grubs. He showed Brent a stem he collected with an abnormal, round-shaped growth. Upon slicing it open, out crawled a white grub. It was a small guy but apparently worked based on how many bluegills were laying on the ice.

As Sam's fishing trip attendance became less frequent, Brent began going to the lake on his own or with friends. Having no driver's license and sometimes no wax worms in the refrigerator, a stop in the goldenrod patch was easier than a long walk to a bait shop near Lake Lansing. However, this trick only worked early in the season, as woodpeckers or other parasites would eventually deplete the resource.

Steve Armstrong, a long-time friend and authority on natural areas surrounding Mud Lake, frequently accompanied Brent to catch his share of panfish. Steve lived on Coral Way, the next street east of Brent, and being the same age, the two frequently spent spare time together. They regularly ran with the "neighborhood gang" as well, which included boys and girls of various ages. Steve's three older brothers conditioned him into a tougher than normal kid by directing their aggressions his way. With both parents working and leaving the foursome unattended during the day, Steve withstood multiple tortures dished out by his elders. Since Brent spent so much time with Steve, he was often captured and held down for a pink belly or sternum knuckling just for showing up—all in playful fun, but sometimes quite intense.

Aside from this rough stuff, the family was tightly bonded. Steve could be away doing family things at any time, unannounced to the neighborhood kids. Being gone for an afternoon in early May and returning with morel mushroom-filled bags from the Woods happened more than once, with no hints about exactly where they were found.

Steve, Brent, and Jim Deemer, another youngster, one year older, who lived across the street from Brent, led the younger neighborhood gang members when the group coalesced. Their activities almost always involved competition. It could be an organized game like wiffle ball or football, or simple contests to determine who could run the fastest, jump the farthest, or successfully complete a daring stunt.

One of the neighborhood's backyard trees offered an ideal structure to hold daredevil events. It was a multi-stemmed boxelder with five individual trunks ascending from its base, all leaning slightly away from the tree's center. The distance between each trunk gradually became greater as trunk height increased. Well-placed lateral branches on every trunk made for easy climbing. Since the gang spent a lot of time in this tree, games were invented that involved jumping from trunk to trunk. Easy jumps at low elevations allowed several kids to orbit around the tree in a one-way direction, all at one time. The higher jumps were only done by the most daring, and new, more difficult jumps were always under consideration.

Steve was the jump master, capable of soaring long distances from one trunk to the next at over 20 feet above the ground. His fearless nature and inherent athletic ability placed him well above everyone else in tree jump contests. Yet he relentlessly coaxed others to match his skills—particularly Jim and Brent. Jim was most likely to answer his challenge. On one attempt to prove his daring demeanor, Jim's grip slips loose from the landing branch. Like missing a grab for a swinging trapeze, his body rotates to a horizontal position before dropping straight down. Luckily, a kid's clubhouse occupied a spot about 10 feet below his fall, where the house roof catches him landing flat on his back. After about a minute, Jim got his wind back enough to talk and convinced the others that nothing was broken. Once on his feet, the games continued.

The tree was like a family or friends' group where, over time, individuals (the trunks) grew further apart. The jumping boys' successful circular movement relied on trusting relationships with each other and a continuous connective energy between them and the trunks. When a relationship was pushed too far, breaking the energy connection, pain was felt throughout the group, especially where the relationship broke. But after healing, trust and the relationships continued with more caution. As the boys grew older and stopped making jumps in the tree, individual trunks continued growing apart but were always connected by their roots until the tree died.

Steve and Brent's relationship continued outside of the boxelder tree in many structured circles including team sports and school activities. In eighth grade, they partnered on an end-of-year project in woodshop class that involved making a jon boat. It was a usable watercraft constructed primarily of one four-by-eight sheet of exterior-grade plywood. Two 16-inch-wide by eight-foot-long pieces were cut from the sheet for the boat's side panels, leaving one wider piece for the boat's bottom. This piece was pulled upward on the front end to match a curve that was cut away from both side panels. Ribbing, a prow, a transom, and seats were added with a lot of glue and overnight clamping. The craft was finished in a glossy sky blue that dried just in time to drag it home on the last day of school. With the school no longer holding end-of-year picnics at Lake Lansing Amusement Park, this event was a welcome celebratory substitute.

Figure 5.1. Boat made from exterior grade plywood.

In earlier years on the last day of school, kids from the fourth through eighth grades were given a couple free tickets for rides at the park and were discharged at 10:00 a.m. to jump on the bus. With the park only a few blocks away, a bus was not necessary, although it was a good idea to keep the kids together as a group. Once at the park, everyone was on their own, but they were instructed to catch a departing bus in the early afternoon for a ride back to school where regular bus runs to the outskirts of town would be available. Only responsible kids living in the farmlands caught the gist of this and remembered to catch the return buses. They still had an incredible day—just a little shorter than the town kids.

When arriving at the park, pandemonium broke out. Absolute excitement consumed everyone. Screams of terror and delight blended with the noise of gasoline-powered generators, carousel music, and the Cyclone roller coaster thundering against its track on every descent. First-time riders on this beast were terrified beyond description, while experienced ones chose to go no-handed, holding their arms straight up above their heads. The slow ascent up the tallest, first hill paired with a steady clanking of metal against the track instilled riders with utter panic. Once at the top, the train of cars circled a curve shrouded by treetops and then, with no chance of turning back, dropped vertically downward, so fast and steeply it seemed to leave the track. The feeling of being airborne immediately transitioned to that of extreme pressure, cramming bodies against their seats when rounding the hill's bottom. And before one could recover, it started all over again, and again. This continued as the cars left the park's center ground through and out of the tree canopy, into a grassy field, before a return trip that was just as brutal. Breathless and windblown bodies slumping in their places when the cars arrived back at the boarding gate let the next riders in line know this ride will be great!

Figure 5.2. Spinning tilt-a-whirl cars were fixed to a platform that rotated over humps and bumps.
Image credit: © Bill Duchaine –USA TODAY NETWORK

For hours, kids wandered tirelessly from ride to ride. Near the giant roller coaster, airplanes flew around a central pole dangling from steel cables attached to steel beams. Being most everyone's favorite ride, small fuselages were equipped with manually operated wings. Kids could control the height of flight by rotating the wing position using a grab handle on the wing's edge above the cockpit. Legend has it that Doug Aper flew his plane so high it collided with an oak tree adjacent to the ride area, which explained why his arm was in a cast for the rest of the summer.

Next to the airplanes, the giant Ferris wheel relentlessly lured its patrons by repeating its vertical rotation, stopping only to load and unload passengers. Seats were equipped with latching grab bars providing riders with something to wrap their white knuckles around when finding themselves at the top of the wheel. Here, it would suddenly stop, swinging the seat to and fro, seeming capable of dumping its payload onto the plaza far below.

Hot dogs, french fries, and cotton candy replaced the everyday lunch menu. The fries were like no other—cooked in a special oil that must have only been supplied to this park (or maybe left over from last summer). Plastic squeeze bottles of vinegar were provided to mitigate any ill effects. Although this did nothing to protect against barfing on an after-lunch Tilt-A-Whirl ride.

The trips to Lake Lansing Amusement Park were hard to beat, but Brent and Steve thought their handcrafted water toy matched up pretty well. Unfortunately, the heat of a typical June afternoon made the trek home quite agonizing. The boat was not light and was more easily dragged than carried. This worked okay through lawns, but they carefully lifted it over roads and driveways to avoid damaging the hull's finish. At about the halfway mark, they decided to change course and veer off toward Mud Lake. This would avoid going all the way home and later backtracking with the heavy load.

Finding an access path through someone's backyard on Biscayne Way would be necessary for the delivery, so they abandoned the boat along the roadside to scout out the best route. After finding last year's footpath, the boat was retrieved for the final pull. Tall grass and rough terrain complicated the effort, and with sweat dripping from their bodies, they were magnets for deer flies. Finally, a safe hiding place was found on the edge of the marsh—good enough for the time being. Since they had no paddle, poles, or bait with them, there would be no fishing that day—only pleasant reminiscing about how they used to celebrate the last day of school with snow cones and rides on the roller coaster at Lake Lansing Amusement Park.

Steve and Brent enjoyed a couple of boat fishing trips that summer but not to the extent they had expected. Two people in this tiny boat casting fishhooks was a challenge, and summer jobs along with activities involving teenage girls started happening, which cut into time for Mud Lake. With high school beginning in the fall, attending summer dances opened their eyes to a whole new set of friends that seemed disinterested in sloshing through a marsh. At the end of the summer, Steve dragged the boat home for storage behind his garage, where it stayed for several years. Here, it was in plain sight of the garbage man, who eventually offered to buy it. Steve accepted, and that ended any further summer fishing on Mud Lake.

References

Telephone Interviews and E-mail Correspondence With Bridget Booth, Certified Environmental Educator, Teacher at Haslett Middle School (Mar. 2 - Apr. 22, 2022).

From the Archives: Lake Lansing Amusement Park, LANSING STATE J. (Aug. 24, 2015), https://www.lansingstatejournal.com/story/news/local/2015/08/21/archives-lake-lansing-amusement-park/32142727/.

WKAR Specials: Things Not Here Anymore—1995 (PBS television broadcast Mar. 30, 1995), http://video.wkar.org/video/2199703945 (edited for YouTube: *Haslett History—Lake Lansing Amusement Park*, YOUTUBE (Sept. 25, 2013), https://www.youtube.com/watch?v=sKKO9UIhb7g).

Chapter 6
New Kids on the Block

Activity surrounding Mud Lake continued to escalate during the 1960s, even though Steve and Brent were finding new endeavors. Lakeview Heights harbored plenty of younger kids primed for experiencing their own explorations. The Hagenbuch family constructed their home at the far west end of Biscayne Way in the early 1960s on one of two lots left vacant after all the one-story ranches were built. Difficulties imposed by the adjacent wetland in constructing the house explained why these lots were left vacant. Although once completed, the site provided the family with a spectacular gateway to amenities surrounding Mud Lake.

Rod and LaVerne Hagenbuch both graduated from Haslett High School, two years apart. LaVerne grew up in a small house next to the railroad tracks just south of Lake Lansing, while Rod resided on a farm next to the same railroad several miles east of town. Their early married life happened in a basement apartment offered by LaVerne's parents, where Beth and her older brother Kris were born, before moving to the new house on Biscayne. So, as Steve, Brent, and their buddies approached high school graduation, the Hagenbuch kids and their friends were just getting their feet wet with Mud Lake fun.

Nestled into the crook of the Woods rounding the outside corner of the neighborhood, the Hagenbuch lot sloped to the south down to the marshy outer reach of Mud Lake. Their yard, being a little lower than the rest of the development, offered a quick descent to the marsh. Beth's earliest outdoor encounters, at about three years old, were anchored around the marsh edge, embraced by leafy trees and wildlife in the Woods. Floor-to-ceiling family room windows enframed the marshy woodland, creating a natural backdrop for indoor life as well. Her experiences in the outdoors gradually expanded as she trailed behind her brother and played in the company of next-door friends.

The landscape offered continually changing grounds to stimulate imagination and provided physical challenges for kids to test and conquer—a rich interaction with the natural world. An endless supply of frogs and tadpoles, minnows and garter snakes, snails, toads, bats, birds, possums, raccoons, bunnies, chipmunks, and squirrels were a daily part of their lives. The Woods even gifted the family with a stray kitten rescued by Kris with tender concern and exuberant excitement to have a real kitten. For over 20 years, Smokey was house cat by day and hunter by night, enjoying a steady diet of all that lived just outside the house doors.

The wet marsh of Mud Lake seeped up to the southern edge of their backyard. The ground edging against the lawn was black and wet. The air from this area was scented with rich and sometimes ripe dampness, releasing unrelenting waves of backyard mosquitos during the summer. If one ventured into this band of trees where marsh met housing development, a dark muck sucked at your shoes, and a tangle of undergrowth grabbed at ankles and legs. It was deterrent enough to redirect organized play activities elsewhere but wonderful enough, in its dangerous ways, to attract spontaneous, unstructured excitement—like going solo in skipping from a tiny dry footing to a treacherous log, through thickets and back, or to serve as a delightful challenge for small gangs of kids, boasting of bravery, with the potential of becoming hilariously soaked and dirty in the end.

A path coming from within the Woods opened at the far edge of the Hagenbuchs' front lawn. A small pond laid just inside this threshold where Kris and Beth spent much of their time. Beth aspired to keep up with Kris as long as he would tolerate, but she was equally content to explore on her own, squatting at the water's edge prodding the murky water, navigating her steps along the pond's perimeter, examining small things in the leaf litter, or making her own way over and under fallen logs and branches through the Woods when Kris roamed farther afield.

Figure 6.1. Small pond just inside the Woods where Beth prodded at the murky water.

LaVerne had a love of the outdoors and a fearless spirit when it came to catching frogs, handling worms, snakes, and floppy fish, or inviting a slug to slide across her hand. As an actress in local theater productions, she performed her role of teaching the art of not being squeamish or afraid of the outdoors with the appropriate flair and drama to capture the kids' attention. Her audience, however, Beth and Kris, was less enthusiastic, observing but usually declining to participate.

Even so, LaVerne's impromptu lessons imparted an attitude of embracing the natural world and practicing bravery in outdoor play. Kris and Beth were purposely given free rein to wander and explore with their friends. Adults were always nearby with most moms at home, reliably calling at dinnertime every night. There were no experienced hunters, fishers, campers, or naturalists guiding their outdoor experiences. They largely roamed unsupervised.

During the 1960s the O'Bryant farm occupied the area west of Mud Lake, separated from the Woods by a fence extending west toward Marsh Road. Early play mostly happened on the higher ground and in the ponds of the Woods. Mud Lake seemed inaccessible beyond the fence and marsh. Trespassing onto the farm was also said to be "off limits" by mom and dad, yet cows occasionally crashed the fence and feasted on LaVerne's backyard garden. In retaliation, while hanging over the wire fence to watch the cows, the neighborhood gang could not resist taunting the bull when he was in the field. Nothing matched the inevitable frightened, excited, and joyous running away when his massive and dangerous attention was caught.

The corner of Biscayne Way and Woodville Road was inundated with children. Outdoor fun and social interactions were continuous. Friendships, rivalries, shifting alliances, and play were interwoven with the street, the Woods, Mud Lake, and its marsh—all a constant presence and playground throughout years of growing up together.

Some of Beth's closest playmates lived next door. Lori Garver lived across the street, and the girls remained friends into adulthood. Kris' pals included several living up Woodville and down Biscayne. The core group often played together in raucous games of kick the can, hide-and-seek, races, touch football, baseball, biking, and skateboarding. New games would be made up when in smaller groups, negotiating rules and roles, arguing, compromising, roaming, and inventing. The group walked to school together, joining in a stream of classmates through the Woods along the way.

During Beth's early life and elementary school years, she rarely engaged with Mud Lake surroundings beyond what was called "the swamp" in her backyard. Life and play mostly took place in the yard, on the street, in the Woods, and at school. Girl life in the 1960s remained influenced by gender-specific thinking of the 1950s. Besides her time in the swamp, demands included dolls, Barbies and their wardrobes, sewing, baking, indoor chores, ballet lessons, summer swim team, piano lessons, flute lessons, and Brownies.

Daylong excursions into the marsh were tough to schedule. So, the woods at the edge of the yard served as a source of retreat—a peace and connection to nature that permeated her life from her earliest childhood days. The normal rhythms of suburban life laid open brief pockets of time when the Woods belonged to her, times when families were at home, early in the morning, around the dinner hour, and warm summer nights of stolen play before bedtime. During these times, when the hum of neighborhood activity and frenetic social energy released by gangs of kids was calmed, her experience was mostly personal, independent, and introspective. She inhabited the Woods and the edge of the marsh as a wanderer, an observer, and perhaps an explorer of smaller things. Her experiences lacked the dramatic adventures undertaken by her brother but left her brimming with impressionistic and sensory memories—immersed in the landscape, the mirror-like glint off the brown-green pond surface, jellylike tadpoles, patterns of branches, textures of wood and bark, sounds, scents, and so on.

In contrast, Kris became a veteran in exploration and daring adventures in the marsh and Mud Lake with battle scars to prove it. He and neighboring Randy Budzynski found success in summer fishing, taking the catch to Randy's where his mother, Jo, master cook, would fry it up, sometimes having dinner parties to serve their fish. However, bluegills were not her favorite—too small. Rumors floated the neighborhood of a 54-inch northern pike with three-inch-long teeth that they had to club to death with a log. Whatever the reality, the pike satisfied Jo's craving for larger fish.

Reference

Telephone Interviews and E-mail Correspondence With Beth Hagenbuch (Feb. 11 - Apr. 5, 2022).

Chapter 7
Other Things Happening Surrounding Mud Lake

With all this excitement around Mud Lake, other things actually happened in the world that competed for the spotlight. One notable event in February 1962 involved Colonel John Glenn, who orbited the earth three times in outer space. Although highly regarded for his bravery, he spoke lightly of this virtue. Regarding taking risks, Glenn would tell the story of climbing a giant sycamore tree in his childhood. "Every time I climbed that tree, I forced myself to climb to the last possible safe limb and look down," staring down 55 feet to the ground. "Every time I did it, I told myself I'd never do it again. But I kept going back because it scared me, and I had to know I could overcome that."

When asked about the view to earth while in orbit from Friendship 7, his response over the radio was simple: "Oh, that view is tremendous." He later expressed his amazement over the brilliant-colored sunsets and his gratitude for experiencing four of them in one day. In a more visionary statement, he explained how we are on the brink of expanded knowledge about ourselves and our surroundings that is beyond description or comprehension at this time. Kids near Mud Lake memorialized Glenn's achievements by naming a show of skill with a yo-yo, involving three spins overhead in sleeper mode, the "John Glenn."

Later the same year, Rachel Carson's book, *Silent Spring,* was published, which identified an urgent need to protect the environment. Considered the book that initiated global grassroots of the environmental movement, it focused on the negative effects of pesticides that were an integral part of U.S. agriculture. She noted the harmful effects that DDT inflicted on bird populations and warned of a future spring without singing birds. The book provided parents living around Mud Lake with factual content explaining why bald eagle sightings were becoming rare.

Three years later, Carson released *The Sense of Wonder*, sparking a new purpose for people to spiritually connect with nature. To quote from this book:

> Those who dwell among the beauties and mysteries of the earth are never alone or weary of life. Those who contemplate the beauty of the earth find reserves of strength that will endure as long as life lasts. The more clearly we can focus our attention on the wonders and realities of the universe, the less taste we shall have for destruction.

The "Students for a Democratic Society" emerged during this time, largely out of the University of Michigan, with goals of ending racial injustice and addressing problems of poverty and impoverished neighborhoods. Yet due to their activism and protesting about university academic policies, they were perceived as a new radical leftist movement, particularly after their focus shifted toward protesting the Vietnam War, which plagued the decade.

In 1963, Bob Dylan first performed his call-to-action song, "The Times They Are A-Changin'," during his concert opener in New York City at Carnegie Hall. The lyrics focused on the frustrations of youth and the Civil Rights Movement. A memorable phrase from this song urged people to do something about current issues or there would be consequences:

If your time to you is worth savin'
Then you better start swimmin' or you'll sink like a stone

This was just the beginning of a long career that led to Dylan's recognition as one of the world's greatest musical artists. His awards, such as the Presidential Medal of Freedom and the Nobel Prize for Literature, prove the depth of his legacy. Amazingly, his lyrics written in the '60s are just as moving today as they were in his early heyday. Some of these include:

When you got nothing, you got nothing to lose
—"Like a Rolling Stone," 1965

So when you see your neighbor carryin' somethin'
Help him with his load
And don't go mistaking Paradise
For that home across the road
—"The Ballad of Frankie Lee and Judas Priest," 1967

Why wait any longer for the one you love
When he's standing in front of you
—"Lay, Lady, Lay," 1969

With the events of the early 1960s recognized by many as what could be openings into a new and exciting era, simultaneous incidents and several that followed turned the decade upside down. Those who were clinging onto values from the 1950s were noticeably out of sync, yet they instilled a formidable force in the business world and in government, which likely induced at least some of the following occurrences.

- Marilyn Monroe, a glamorous Hollywood icon, was found dead in her Los Angeles bungalow bedroom at age 36. Toxicology results showed elevated levels of chloral hydrate, likely from her sleeping pills, implying she died by suicide. With disbelief among her friends, theories surfaced involving a wide range of homicide motives including some involving Robert and John Kennedy. Seeming like something out of a movie, the Mud Lake neighborhood dismissed the event simply as another Hollywood thing, although copies of *Playboy* magazine containing nude photos of Marilyn were saved in obscure places by some boys and dads. An investigation into her death reopened in 1982 with no new conclusions. Yet doubt regarding the documented cause of her death still remains among many.
- U.S. military advisors assisted a puppet government in South Vietnam in defending against a nationalist movement to regain control of their country following decades of French control. This evolved into a decade-long war killing more than 58,000 U.S. troops, finally ending in 1975. Early in the conflict, when it seemed insignificant, Vietnamese currency somehow filtered into the hands of kids living near Mud Lake, making highly prized objects when trading marbles, agates, and postage stamps.
- School children conducted practice drills on how to survive a nuclear bomb attack, while home improvement projects often involved building underground bomb shelters. Although horrifically loud military planes often rumbled across the sky in these days, all flights were conducted by U.S. forces, and no bombs were dropped. Yet these occurrences invariably caused head-turns to the southeast to verify no mushroom cloud loomed over Detroit. The Hagenbuch home, typical of new-house construction, came equipped with a reinforced concrete, basement bomb shelter to protect the family from incoming Russian missiles. Otherwise known as the playroom, it also provided the place to wait out tornado warnings. Other effective uses for these shelters included storing potatoes, canned goods, and wine.

- President John F. Kennedy was gunned down by Lee Harvey Oswald as Kennedy rode in a presidential motorcade through Dealey Plaza in downtown Dallas. Soon afterwards, Jack Ruby killed Oswald on live TV with a bullet to his stomach, as Oswald was escorted through the basement of the Dallas police headquarters, on his way to a more secure county jail. Following a period of mourning, a stunned nation was consumed with conspiracy theories about who killed Kennedy. Like Marilyn's death, his assassination remains a source of bewilderment, controversy, and speculation.
- Dr. Martin Luther King Jr. stood on the second-floor balcony of the Lorraine Motel in Memphis, when a sniper's bullet struck him in the neck. He was pronounced dead about an hour later, at age 39. Shock and distress over this news ignited racial tension and sparked rioting in more than 100 U.S. cities, including burning and looting, with nearby Detroit being one of the most affected. Since many Mud Lake area families had relatives living in Detroit, this tragic chain of events imposed personal concerns.
- Robert F. Kennedy took several killing bullets from Sirhan Sirhan at the Ambassador Hotel in Los Angeles shortly after winning the California presidential primary and announcing the country was ready to end its fractious divisions. At that time, Kennedy was widely perceived as the only person in American politics capable of uniting the people.
- Malcolm X was assassinated while delivering a speech in Manhattan's Audubon Ballroom. With childhood roots in Lansing, not far from Mud Lake, Malcolm became a spokesman for the Nation of Islam, a separatist organization that preached Black self-reliance and empowerment, not integration, and condemned whites as immoral "devils." After making a religious pilgrimage to Mecca in 1964, his reappraisal of whites mellowed his approach for fighting oppression to become much less abrasive. His change of heart and speaking out against Nation of Islam leaders provoked their members to shoot him dead.

Simon and Garfunkel summed things up in 1964 when they recorded "The Sound of Silence." The song expresses the anguish experienced by youth, evoked by feelings of alienation. In the early '60s, this was brought on by society's inability to communicate effectively due to not talking and not listening, combined with a willing acceptance of thought and opinion provided by mass media—like blindly following a demagogue in today's world.

With the Beatles dominating popular music, only 2,000 records of the song sold when first released, causing Simon and Garfunkel to go their separate ways. However, Columbia Records producer Tom Wilson added drums and electric instruments to the acoustic track and rereleased it, making it a huge hit that reunited the duo. Over the long run, the acoustic version received more continuous radio play, and due to its simple, appealing melody it eventually became a classic that remains relevant today. Unfortunately, not many older folks living in the mid-1960s were changed by the song's lyrics, and as differing opinions between young and old became more widespread, it wouldn't be long before an entire generation rejected their parents' middle-class values.

As the war in Vietnam escalated, so did tensions between public camps. Songwriter Paul Simon's messaging about our society's inability to effectively communicate was dead right, as represented by increasing battlefield casualties. War protests by young people became common, but were going unheard until January 1968, when North Vietnam launched their Tet Offensive. Tet is a culturally important celebration of the Lunar New Year, and the U.S. military was unprepared when the North Vietnamese and Vietcong used Tet festivities as cover, surging into Saigon and other key cities. U.S. forces regained control of most areas within days, although a battle for Hue raged on for nearly a month. During this battle, U.S. troops discovered mass graves containing thousands of people who had been executed during the Communist occupation during and after Tet. Although the offensive was a military disaster for the Vietcong, with 37,000 dead, the United States lost 2,500 men, undermining public support for the war and giving the Vietcong a political victory.

CBS news anchor Walter Cronkite, known as "the most trusted man in America," conducted a special broadcast on the situation after his own experience of following intensive combat in the aftermath of the offensive. Cronkite shared his personal feelings, telling viewers, "It is more certain than ever that the bloody experience of Vietnam is to end in a stalemate." This was seen as a key factor in then-President Lyndon Johnson's decision to offer negotiations and to not seek reelection in 1968.

This was the year sentiments about the war began shifting for many in the Mud Lake area. Young people in particular, like Steve and Brent, could no longer accept opinions handed down by their World War II veteran dads. Anti-war music streamed from their radios. Clothing purposely appeared rebellious, and part of being cool meant following current trends. This included marijuana use, which became easier to acquire than beer. With

Brent's long hair being an explosive point of contention, dinnertime discussions about the validity of the war (or almost anything) could rarely be conducted without a shouting match erupting about hair length.

Two months following the Tet Offensive, the Charlie Company, 11th Brigade, was on a "search and destroy" mission in the hamlet of My Lai. Something went horribly wrong, resulting in violent death for hundreds of unarmed civilians, including women, children, and the elderly. News of massacres at My Lai did not reach public media until November 1969, yet when aired, the atrocity resonated an overwhelming question to the American public about our motive for continuing the war.

This news came only one month after two million U.S. citizens staged the one-day Peace Moratorium—the largest demonstration in our history. Protestors included many first-time activists. Religious services, street rallies, public meetings, school seminars, and marches were conducted around the nation, as more than 250,000 demonstrators flooded Washington, D.C. Participants wore black armbands to signify opposition to the war and to honor the dead.

The anti-war movement was particularly strong on college campuses. At nearby Michigan State University, students protested by camping outside in tents and holding sit-ins to close Grand River Avenue, the main drag through downtown East Lansing. After taunting lines of riot gear-equipped policemen, sprinting to safety triggered emotions similar to escaping from the O'Bryant farm bull. Although many young people saw the war as a form of unchecked authority, which they resented, other Americans viewed government opposition as unpatriotic and treasonous—a country divided.

In 1970, U.S. and South Vietnamese forces invaded Cambodia, targeting the opposition's supply bases. The South Vietnamese also invaded Laos but were forced back by North Vietnam. These invasions, which were in violation of international law, fueled more rebellious intensity on college campuses across America. At Kent State University in Ohio, National Guardsmen shot and killed four students. Two students at Jackson State University in Mississippi were killed by police at another protest 10 days later. The Peace Moratorium followed by these events started waking up hard-liners in support of the war's continuation. Why are we killing our kids over this? Even Steve's and Brent's dads were getting it.

Although public sentiment in favor of the war diminished, it lingered on for six more years under the direction of President Richard Nixon. He believed ending the war honorably was essential to the success of his presidency and the American people would give him the necessary time to get this done. To accomplish his goal, Nixon directed the U.S. military to escalate pressure on the battlefield during his first months in office. Simultaneously, he offered conciliatory terms in newly begun negotiations, and urged the Soviet Union to encourage their North Vietnamese allies to be agreeable. However, none of this brought him closer to ending the war. To appease the American people, Nixon began withdrawing forces. As U.S. troop strength and capabilities declined, the United States assisted South Vietnam in building up their military force through a program known as "Vietnamization." However, there was never any indication that South Vietnam could develop the necessary combat capability required to defend against the North Vietnamese on their own.

With no luck in persuading all parties to negotiate, Nixon ordered massive B-52 bomb attacks on the North Vietnamese heartland, which eventually brought their leaders to sign a peace agreement in January 1973. This settlement enabled the United States to withdraw from the war and welcome American prisoners of war back home. However, neither of the Vietnamese parties upheld the agreement, and the war continued. To stop the conflict, Nixon threatened to recommit B-52s to combat but never followed through due to a combination of factors including domestic and congressional reluctance to re-engage in the war, economic constraints, and the Watergate scandal, which increasingly distracted Nixon. Finally, in March 1975, after Nixon resigned from office, North Vietnamese forces launched a major offensive, and on April 30, 1975, North Vietnamese Army tanks rolled through the gate of the presidential palace in Saigon, ending the war.

The 20-year-long conflict beginning with an independence movement by Vietnam against French colonial rule was over. The United States supported France, based on a World War II alliance, and eventually inherited the war. Young Americans died for a cause they did not initiate, and those who did not participate were left with feelings of guilt confused by thankfulness for not going. In the end, there was no mark in the win column, as President Nixon had pursued—only a feeling of emptiness and a nation's desire to move on, which did not benefit surviving soldiers or the people fighting to bring them home. It was a wound to everyone living through it that hasn't entirely healed.

Oddly enough, all developed nations of today are caught up in a battle against nature that began nearly 200 years ago. Like what happened with Vietnam, they are now in so deep, it is hard to get out. Sadly, it's another unwinnable quest that has taken the lives of thousands who had no involvement in starting or perpetuating the movement, and it will likely kill millions more as time goes on. The resistance against limiting the use of fossil fuels will be further discussed in upcoming chapters.

As the 1970s unfolded, children seeking change in the early 1960s had grown into young adults. Worn down by a government unwilling to compromise on fundamental issues of human rights and dignity, many dropped out. The distractions of a drug culture lurking beyond marijuana eased this decision for those with no clear direction. Others became less impassioned with protesting as they transitioned into a world of adult responsibilities. Still, some remained vigilant, but with the war coming to an end, so did the most important reason to make a stand.

After two years of college beginning in 1970, Brent's grade point average dangerously declined, yet he still showed up for class, and a new understanding that more time needed to be applied toward studies became clear if he was to remain in school. With Kris just beginning high school, his outdoor life was daring, pushing boundaries and adventurous—still making trips to Mud Lake, which became more accessible after the property transitioned to Haslett Public schools. While at home, he mostly existed in the bomb shelter turned male teenage hideout with Midnight, his black lab and loyal companion, and rock music on his record player. He and Beth spent less time together. The more studious life of his nerdy sister included many trips to Mud Lake but with more cerebral parameters.

The environmental movement sparked by Rachel Carson appeared to stand still for over a decade due to Beatlemania, assassinations, hippies, and the Vietnam War controversy flooding the news media. However, significant discussions continued in response to worsening environmental conditions with some good results. The nation's water quality was in dire straits, which became the focus of attention.

Lake Erie was declared dead in 1965. Smothered in pollution, it was becoming a stinking, slime-covered mess—a 10,000-square-mile dead lake, possibly past the point of no return. River water quality in urban areas deteriorated so badly that in October 1969, the Rouge River, near Detroit, caught on fire due to oil floating on its surface. At that time, it was considered minor news since this river had long been accepted as a lost cause. After all, industrial pollutants had to go somewhere! In the 1940s and '50s, "the solution to pollution was dilution." From 1946 to 1948, nearly six million gallons of oil and other petroleum products were discharged into the Rouge and Detroit Rivers each year.

In June of that same year, Cleveland's Cuyahoga River caught on fire for at least the 12th time; the first fire ignited in 1868. Like the Rouge River, the Cuyahoga was almost always covered in oil since its industrialization shortly after the Civil War, and its bubbling stench unfortunately became an accepted symbol of the times. Bloated rats among other dead things occasionally floated through the mess, and accidental body contact was cause for an immediate hospital visit. Everyone knew it was polluted, but pollution meant industry was thriving—a sign of economic success.

Figure 7.1. Photo of 1952 Cuyahoga River fire accompanying Time Magazine*'s article, which contributed to establishing the Environmental Protection Agency and the Clean Water Act.*

Image credit: Getty Images

Like the Rouge fire, the Cuyahoga fire initially drew little attention—it was just another Cuyahoga River fire. However, an article in *Time* magazine followed with a dramatic photo showing flames leaping up from the water, engulfing a tugboat. It was actually a photo of a more serious 1952 fire, since no picture of the 1969 fire was known to exist, but it caught the public's attention. Ironically, Cleveland's residents had already initiated steps to restore the river based on new ideas associated with what would become known as "environmentalism." Regardless, Cleveland was becoming a symbol of environmental degradation, which was reinforced by the *Time* article and river pollution publicity created by the city's mayor, Carl Stokes, the first Black mayor of a major city when elected in 1967. Using Cleveland's flawed environmental standing as ammo, Mayor Stokes and his brother, U.S. Representative Louis Stokes, testified before Congress to urge greater federal involvement in pollution control, which significantly influenced the establishment of the U.S. Environmental Protection Agency in 1970 and the passing of the federal Clean Water Act of 1972.

The Clean Water Act significantly upgraded the Federal Water Pollution Control Act of 1948, which had almost no effect. Focusing on water quality, the 1972 Act sets minimum standards for industrial waste discharges and provides regulations for problems like toxic chemical and oil spills. The Act was further improved in 1987 by removing its original construction grant program and replacing it with the streamlined State Water Pollution Control

Revolving Fund. It was later amended to address wetlands protection and Great Lakes water quality.

As one result of this legislation, the Cuyahoga River's water quality improved during following decades, and business investors capitalized by converting an abandoned industrial landscape into an entertainment district featuring restaurants, nightclubs, and music venues. Similarly, the Rouge River saw greatly reduced industrial discharges, which started to improve its water quality. To further restore the river, Wayne County officials spent more than one billion dollars to eliminate combined sewer overflows and complete other restoration work. With $345 million funded by the federal government, largely through a grant known as the Rouge River Wet Weather Demonstration Project, local match dollars and in-kind services covered remaining expenses. Where almost no life existed in water that was considered unsafe to touch, the Rouge now supports 65 species of fish and has facilities to launch kayaks!

On another up note, the U.S. surgeon general released a landmark report in 1964 stating that smoking is hazardous to human health, contradicting decades of tobacco advertising that suggested health benefits are gained from smoking. With a requirement for this warning to be printed on every cigarette package, it would be two decades before most people took the message seriously—possibly because of the tumultuous times during the 1960s and early '70s or maybe due to larger print on cigarette packaging like LSMFT—Lucky Strike Means Fine Tobacco.

References

Lorraine Boissoneault, *The Cuyahoga River Caught Fire at Least a Dozen Times, but No One Cared Until 1969*, Smithsonian Mag. (June 19, 2019), https://www.smithsonianmag.com/history/cuyahoga-river-caught-fire-least-dozen-times-no-one-cared-until-1969-180972444/.

Sarah E. Boslaugh, *Silent Spring—Work by Carson*, Britannica, https://www.britannica.com/topic/Silent-Spring (last updated Apr. 18, 2023).

Edoardo Crasta, *The Sound of Silence: The Meaning of Simon and Garfunkel's Masterpiece*, Auralcrave (Aug. 27, 2020), https://auralcrave.com/en/2020/08/27/the-sound-of-silence-the-meaning-of-simon-and-garfunkels-masterpiece/.

Shaunacy Ferro, *9 Moving Quotes From Pioneering Astronaut John Glenn*, Mental Floss (Dec. 8, 2016), https://www.mentalfloss.com/article/89778/9-moving-quotes-pioneering-astronaut-john-glenn.

Friends of the Rouge, *Species of Fish Found in the Rouge River*, https://therouge.org/species-of-fish-found-in-the-rouge-river/ (last visited May 31, 2023).

John Hartig, *Great Lakes Moment: Rouge River Revived*, Great Lakes Now (Oct. 7, 2022), https://www.greatlakesnow.org/2022/10/great-lakes-moment-rouge-river-revived/.

History, *This Day in History: Dr. Martin Luther King Jr. Is Assassinated*, https://www.history.com/this-day-in-history/dr-king-is-assassinated (last updated Jan. 18, 2022).

History, *This Day in History: Marilyn Monroe Is Found Dead*, https://www.history.com/this-day-in-history/marilyn-monroe-is-found-dead (last updated Aug. 3, 2021).

History, *This Day in History: President John F. Kennedy Is Assassinated*, https://www.history.com/this-day-in-history/john-f-kennedy-assassinated (last updated Apr. 28, 2023).

History, *This Day in History: Robert F. Kennedy Is Fatally Shot*, https://www.history.com/this-day-in-history/bobby-kennedy-is-assassinated (last updated June 3, 2021).

History, *This Day in History: Malcolm X Assassinated*, https://www.history.com/this-day-in-history/malcolm-x-assassinated (last updated Feb. 19, 2021).

History, *Vietnam War*, https://www.history.com/topics/vietnam-war/vietnam-war-history (last updated Mar. 28, 2023).

Conversations and E-mail Correspondence With Becky Goodman, Downtown Director, City of Petoskey (Feb. 22 - Apr. 28, 2022).

Ronald H. Spector, *Vietnam War*, Britannica, https://www.britannica.com/event/Vietnam-War/Tet-brings-the-war-home (last visited May 31, 2023).

U.S. Environmental Protection Agency, *The Origins of EPA*, https://www.epa.gov/history/origins-epa (last updated June 24, 2022).

Stephanie Vermillion, *14 of Bob Dylan's Most Poignant Lyrics*, Inspiring Quotes, https://www.inspiringquotes.com/bob-dylans-most-poignant-lyrics/YKSLQ3-NggAHrUAD (last visited May 31, 2023).

Chapter 8
More Business Around Mud Lake

The business of conducting ecosystem services at Mud Lake quietly continued without anyone's attention into the 1960s and '70s. Yet today, wetlands of the magnitude that surround Mud Lake are becoming highly recognized and are referred to as nurseries of life because they provide safe habitat for young fish, birds, and other species. Worldwide, more than 5,000 species of plants are found in wetlands, along with one-third of all bird species, 200 species of fish, and 190 species of amphibians. While these nesting, resting, and feeding areas are widely inhabited by common species, many threatened and endangered species make use of them as well. The massive wetland surrounding Mud Lake is no exception.

In addition to providing wildlife habitat, wetlands help stabilize and maintain the water table by acting as sponges. During wet periods, they temporarily contain floodwater and release it slowly, minimizing flood damage. They also serve as a filter system, removing sediment, nutrients, and pollutants from drinking water. Wetlands, like that surrounding Mud Lake, function as sites for groundwater recharge, replenishing and purifying the water in aquifers that supply local wells. Recreational opportunities, such as hunting, fishing, birding, and boating, are another benefit. Probably most importantly, as reported in recent environmental disclosures, they can help with climate change mitigation by sequestering carbon and preventing its release into the atmosphere—a primary cause of climate change. Once carbon is absorbed, wetlands can store it in their water-saturated soils for centuries.

Beth, Kris, Steve, and Brent were oblivious to all the wetland benefits but greatly profited from the lake and its surroundings. The diversion from school and social pressures combined with fresh air and exercise was a health supplement that no one had identified. The kids were taking it only because it was there.

New adventures could be found every day, and as bicycles aided their ability to travel further distances during late elementary and middle school years, larger friend circles expanded throughout the greater Mud Lake area. Orlando Drive housed a group of boys sometimes called the Orlando Street Gang. The name arose out of their involvement in borderline delinquent activities—namely, pumpkin smashing and holiday light disturbance. They called it the "Pumpkin Patrol" and the "Light Legion." A lot of jack-o'-lanterns encountered a messy end along the roadsides after trick-or-treating rituals. Even though far less mischief was noticed by the Light Legion, a few lights were extinguished with a pellet gun. It was a great "tough kid" idea that received more talk than action.

Like Biscayne Way, Orlando Drive borders the marsh around Mud Lake, providing potential lake access. However, during summer, the more expansive wet zone separating Orlando homes from the lake imposes a significant natural barrier. Even so, this did not deter the Orlando Drive boys. The direct connection from their own backyards to the lake diminished the challenge of crossing the marsh. A long walk down Biscayne Way to sneak through an unknown homeowner's land, just to find a shorter way across the marsh, seemed pointless.

In addition to offering picturesque views into the natural area, Orlando Drive presents a pleasant curvature for riding, both horizontally and vertically. Beginning at Biscayne Way, it steeply descends along a gentle bend to the left, then back up and down again, ending at Cornell Road. This unique alignment gave reason for its nickname—Roller Coaster Hill—and it attracted test runs for every wheeled toy in the neighborhood, including bicycles, tricycles, roller skates, wagons, scooters, go-karts, skateboards, pedal cars, minibikes, and more. Bruises and abrasions were common.

The Orlando Street Gang included boys from four families. Dennis Shinn lived at the bottom of the first hill. This prime location offered easy marsh access from his backyard with the bonus of skating opportunities when it froze over. One area, free of plants poking through the ice, called pollywog pond, was large enough to hold neighborhood hockey games. With little knowledge about the game's rules and no adult supervision, injuries commonly occurred. Yet in no way did they impede play when the ice was right. Approaching the top of the next hill, Hank Parker lived on the marsh side of the road with Mark Nimphie on the opposite side. Both homes had wide driveways and basketball hoops, giving endless opportunities for roundball competitions. Near the bottom of the next hill, approaching Cornell Road, Cricket (Chris) Earley's house was next to an empty lot hosting the community water tower and pump house. On this site, water extracted from the aquifer below Mud Lake and surrounding wetland was pressurized by the elevated holding tank for distribution to the immediate area.

The water tower's function went unnoticed by the neighborhood boys, although its sheer height stood out as an incredible climbing challenge. A steel ladder was attached to one of the tower's legs, planting the idea of making a high climb in the minds of the young daredevils. Even though the ladder's first rung was about 20 feet above the ground, this distance provided no hindrance to the experienced climbers of Lakeview Heights. Shinnying up that far was kid stuff, given their training in the Woods, and was a good warm-up for the rest of the climb. At about halfway up the ladder, it was a good idea to not look down, since this was higher than most trees. From there, every rung was carefully gripped before the next pull upward. At the top, a narrow ledge circled the water reservoir, taking the place of John Glenn's last possible safe tree limb before looking down.

The first tower climb was truly terrifying, and like Glenn's sycamore tree climb, it had to be repeated multiple times to lose its impact. Cricket probably did it over 27 times, and Steve, well, who knows? Brent ascended only once, due to the frightful maneuver required when transitioning from the top ledge back to the ladder before going down. By not repeating the climb several more times, his anxiety about heights lingered for decades. And, unfortunately, his one time up was a solo climb with no one watching, so some suspicion encircled his report to the gang. But this was of no concern to Brent, as no doubting criticism could be more uncomfortable than dangling his legs over the tower ledge to find the first ladder rung. The fun ended in the early 1970s when the water tower was removed. Steve and Cricket made good use of their acquired courage and determination—both went on to be state champion wrestlers when in high school, for one example.

By 1969, Beth acquired bicycle mobility and became close friends with Cricket's younger sisters doing indoor things, while Kris connected with Cricket's younger brother, Jim. The boys went into the creek and marsh more than the girls were interested and typically didn't share invitations to their expeditions. Beth was aware of Kris, Jim, and Cricket as they went in and out, but they were mostly out, and her orbit around Orlando Drive came too late to connect with Steve, Brent, or the water tower.

Much later, after the tower's removal, the empty parcel was developed into a township park with a gazebo, a plastic play structure for safe climbing, and a circular strolling path. In 2016, township leaders implemented a "StoryWalk" along the path offering a nontraditional way to get families outdoors, exercising and learning at the same time. Signs were installed along the walkway—each displaying a page from a children's book. When the walkway opened, it featured *Moose on the Loose* and suggested activities for kids to do as they read, although nothing as thrilling as climbing a water tower.

Mark Nimphie was never known to climb the tower, yet he excelled in most everything else—athletically and academically. He and Brent shared a close friendship that intensified with certain activities alternating with long spells of no association. Not all of Mark's and Brent's interests were parallel; ice fishing was not one of Mark's pastimes, although he did hike across the marsh in winter to ice-skate on the lake. Brent noticed an area that was shoveled free of snow from time to time, but they never bumped into one another on the ice.

The school's summer baseball program initially brought them together on a team where Brent caught Mark's ace pitching. That summer they enjoyed a city bus ride to downtown Lansing to see "PT 109"—a matinée movie about John F. Kennedy's heroic time in the U.S. Navy during World War II. Regardless of what Kennedy was doing to lead the country, the movie instilled a compelling bond between young moviegoers and the president, intensifying the shock of his death later that year. After the show, the boys rummaged through Mark's grandmother's basement to find a bunch of old radio tubes and parts that she let Mark take home. The boys spent several days remounting the parts, connecting wires, and plugging and unplugging tubes without any success other than in their minds with a vision of building a radio like what they saw onboard the PT 109.

Following this escapade and summer baseball, they did not connect again until high school, when during the fall of four consecutive years on the gridiron, Mark, the team's quarterback, received the football from between Brent's legs, playing center, to start every offensive play. Beginning as a grueling experience, they lost every game until their senior year when the team won six straight. They would not see each other again until by coincidence after college, during tailgate events at their alma mater. This unplanned meeting in a Michigan State University parking lot happened over several years for no apparent reason other than the annual occurrence of football season.

References

Telephone Interviews and E-mail Correspondence With Chris Earley, Retired Social Worker for the state of Michigan (Mar. 10 - Apr. 14, 2022).

Telephone Interviews and E-mail Correspondence With Beth Hagenbuch, Landscape Architect (Feb. 11 - Apr. 5, 2022).

Telephone Interviews and E-mail Correspondence With Mark Nimphie, Retired Mechanical/ Electrical Engineer (Mar. 5 - Apr. 14, 2022).

Chapter 9
Circling

Circling back to occasionally connect while separately pursuing life experiences continued for Mark and Brent for more than a half century. What is this magic dust that lingers around circular movements? It appears in various ways with every spin. From little movements like kids flying in circles under the canopy of a boxelder tree, to something larger like John Glenn orbiting earth in Friendship 7, each circle resonates a unique energy.

The invisible force field associated with mega circles manifests itself as rings of perpetual motion, many of which are interlocked into circle systems. This web of energized movement creates a framework supporting the survival of all living creatures. Some extra-large circles like the earth revolving around the sun every 365 days and rotating on its own axis every 24 hours are at least partly responsible for life. Other life-support circles include simple movements like the water cycle, where rain falls from the sky to be filtered by the earth while moving below the surface into a lake or stream before evaporating, only to make the loop again.

The circle of life is intertwined with these large circular movements. In this scenario, a "life bean," or whatever the special element is that no one has identified yet, becomes trapped in ordinary materials found on earth for a random duration of time. This infusion results in growth along with potential movement and reproduction. Ultimately, the bean is released at death, rendering the materials lifeless and returning them back to the ground. Meanwhile, any reproductions or descendants of the formerly living material continue the circular movement. Incredible.

And what about the time it takes for the moon to rotate on its axis related to the time it takes to revolve around the earth? These times are exactly equal—roughly 28 days! As a result of these synchronized movements, the moon keeps the same face pointing toward earth. This is truly amazing, although there apparently is a scientific basis for it. Astronomers say this synchronous spin state came about billions of years ago when the same force that creates tides on earth's oceans, the gravitational pull of the moon, acted in reverse. The moon was believed to be spinning much faster in those days than now, and the earth's gravitational pull on its nonperfect circular shape eventually slowed it down to where the fat side of the moon was frozen into position facing us. This force "tidally locked" the two movements—the moon's spin and its revolution around earth—into place with equal time durations. Yeah, right! We should have guessed that.

Without answers for this nighttime marvel during medieval times, it's no wonder that superstitious stories surfaced to justify the strange celestial object that soared across the sky with a slightly different route and shape every night, repeating its sequence every month before disappearing completely for a few nights. Lack of knowledge in any arena often results in superstitions or conspiracy theories to make justifying explanations. The Mayans of Central America believed the moon was an old man lying sideways in the sky. As he turned to face earth, more of his big belly became visible each night until it was full and round. This attracted a jaguar that took bites of his belly every night until he disappeared for three nights to eat and regain strength. Hmm, this sounds reasonable. Most early cultures offered theories about the moon and its changes. Yet long before the moon's changes were understood, people learned how to use its phases as a calendar. They observed the sun and moon having regular cycles, which helped them follow the seasons.

Large, uncomplicated cosmic turns appear to render the most impactful influences on human activity. People have found that by associating a special event with a tick mark on the earth's revolution around the sun, the event's meaning is elevated. Annual celebrations of events or holidays make each occurrence more significant. Circling back to repeat an event after a year passes bakes in a desire to continue doing the event in the following turn of the earth. As recurrences increase, the event becomes tradition. With that achievement, there is no telling when the event will lose its meaning.

Years are a simple result of the earth's movement around the sun, yet time is often regarded as a linear progression, complicating the understanding of time's infinitive quality. When time is regarded as a circular progression, which is consistent with earth's repetitive movement around the sun, it helps to clear up the infinity question and how doing things annually can be extremely powerful. The importance of an event connected to a movement that will go on forever needs no explanation.

In addition to attaching events to celestial circles, people make use of energy emanating from man-made circles, with an early example being the wheel. This simple innovation solved an energy exertion problem and made the impossible become possible. In a more abstract way, "social circles" linking family and friends provide nurturing to our souls and are the building blocks for communities, which are fundamental to our survival. The kids circling under the boxelder is one example where each individual gained personal strength by participating as a group member moving in unison, where, otherwise, they may not risk the danger of flying from trunk to trunk on their own. When kids participate in team sports, they learn how their connected energy elevates their personal abilities, which is critical to a team's success.

In looking closer at these powerful circular movements, waste products are not typically part of the action. For example, there is no cloud of exhaust trailing behind the earth as it travels a familiar path around the sun, and no plastic bottles are left behind when rain falls out of the sky. These movements just continue happening fueled by this invisible, circular energy force without emitting waste. People are beginning to understand how creating waste that cannot be absorbed by our natural systems is problematic—it's clunky, energy-consuming, and not sustainable.

The buildup of unused, visible material, known as solid waste, is a major management issue in populated areas. Plastic waste in particular is emerging as an utmost concern, with tiny plastic particles called "microplastics" now showing up everywhere. These are plastic particles measuring 0.2 inch in diameter or smaller. Nanoplastics are the smallest of these particles and the most worrisome. Like plastic items of any size, these tiny fragments can take thousands of years to decompose while wreaking havoc on the environment. In our Great Lakes and the oceans, these particles are consumed by fish and other aquatic creatures, which can end up on our dinner plates. And, more disturbingly, most water treatment facilities cannot remove all traces of microplastic pollution, so it is showing up in our drinking water. This is why recycling of plastic along with used paper, glass, and metal has become increasingly important. Limiting the use of these materials, particularly in needless packaging or short-use, throwaway items, is another effective way to remove them as a waste product from the human cycle of life, making this cherished movement more sustainable.

Determining what ingredients give rise to "sustainability" remains an ongoing quest. However, large, simplistic moves occurring in nature that don't emit waste offer good examples of what works.

References

Telephone Interviews and E-mail Correspondence With Bridget Booth, Certified Environmental Educator, Science Teacher at Haslett Middle School (Mar. 2 - Apr. 22, 2022).

Sharon J. Huntington, *Myths, Months, and the Moon*, Christian Sci. Monitor (Sept. 17, 2002), https://www.csmonitor.com/2002/0917/p18s01-hfgn.html.

Jay Lamm, *Why Do We See Only One Side of the Moon?*, Irene W. Pennington Planetarium (Oct. 31, 2013), https://penningtonplanetarium.wordpress.com/2013/10/31/why-do-we-see-only-one-side-of-the-moon/.

XiaoZhi Lim, *Microplastics Are Everywhere—But Are They Harmful?*, Nature (May 4, 2021), https://www.nature.com/articles/d41586-021-01143-3.

Chapter 10
A Mud Lake Friend and the Automobile

Another partner typically seen with the Mud Lake neighborhood kids in the 1960s, named Duke, traveled on four legs. This was Brent's dog, a mongrel with beagle and bluetick genes. He stood a little taller than a purebred beagle, and his white socks appeared to be soiled with small brown spots. Otherwise, he sported typical beagle markings but had no idea he was a dog, being a regular member of the neighborhood gang. When greeting his close human friends, he often flashed a "dog smile" by curling his upper lip under itself, exposing his front teeth for a few moments. It could easily have been mistaken for a snarl if not for his tail wag that swung his entire back end.

Duke consumed his weekend breakfasts at several neighboring homes following a paw swipe on their screen doors. His rounds included Steve's house, where he was welcomed in for short visits, belly rubs, and tasty plate scrapings. The Pickens house was another regular stop, where an elderly couple lived with no children remaining at home—just another beagle of sorts, named Deke, which was Duke's best pal when no kids were outside. The Pickens typically offered a bite of toast with peanut butter to both dogs, amused by how they appeared to enjoy licking these goodies off the roofs of their mouths.

Duke, being quite well-behaved unless no one was watching, commonly attended Sunday school, where he took his place in the prone position under the classroom group table. He showed up at the academic schools on occasion but was not allowed to stay long, which was of no concern. His patience for long-winded lectures was short. Straightforward communication like "come here" or "get out of there" was more his style of talk.

His long legs allowed him to keep up to speed on bike trips, although he preferred tagging along on hiking expeditions into the Woods. He was a worthless tree climber but accepted it well—passing time by circling rabbits around the beech and elm trees while his pals did the climbing. He also enjoyed teaming with Brent every day to deliver newspapers. Showing his protective nature, he often wandered way out in front, scouting for any trouble. However, the route included Biscayne Way and Orlando Drive, which both laid adjacent to the Mud Lake area. So, a distracting rabbit could easily lead him into the marsh. When that happened, an hour or so could pass before he would find his way home, in need of some work with the garden hose.

His gentle watchful temperament persisted throughout every day, starting with walking groups of kids up Franklin Street to school. He took the high schoolers first, came back for the junior high crowd, and made a third trip for the elementary school kids. Following a brief nap on the back porch, it all started over for return trips. After-school duties occasionally included supervising marching band practice, making sure Becky tooted her clarinet correctly. Weaving between the marching lines followed by sitting at the field's edge with one cheek puffed out and the tip of his tongue slightly exposed, he showed concern about performing well at the next marching band competition.

As Brent and Steve moved on to high school and became involved with sports, Duke spent increasingly more time on his own, with the Mud Lake marsh being a favored travel destination, not far from the school and adjacent sports fields. Varsity baseball games were played near the marsh on land bordering the scrub shrub area. On one of Duke's spring marsh trips, he sensed a commotion of human activity coming from the school area and decided to investigate. Once out of the brush and into deep center field, he catches a whiff of his buddies—Steve standing near second base and Brent wearing a lot of protective gear behind home plate. A joyful, ear-flopping trot brings him into the infield to greet Steve with his tail wagging and curled-lip smile. But to his surprise, Steve orders him to leave. Recognizing discontent among two nearby groups of people and more people expressing laughter, seated in bleachers behind the ones flailing their arms, Duke decides to check in with Brent at home plate. Rather than continuing his show dog prance, an inconspicuous movement seemed appropriate, so he scooches on his belly, in sneak-mode, past the pitcher's mound into home. Brent removes his catcher's mask, exposing a blushed face, and takes time out to gently hold Duke's cheeks under his ears and explain to him about where spectators need to sit.

After a brief collar drag to the bleachers, Duke joined the group that, for whatever reason, was still laughing. Their chuckling turned into groaning after Duke's swamp odor overtook their senses. With nobody willing to give him a neck massage, Duke eventually became bored with the game and circled behind the bleachers back to the marsh.

After a couple years in high school, Brent abandoned his bicycle and started driving a 1963, brown F-85 Cutlass convertible to get around town. Duke took over the passenger seat when not occupied by Brent's girlfriend, Sue. He knew exactly how to lay his head over the door when the top and/or windows were down to fly his ears—looking cool to all his friends and knowing how his black, white, and brown markings perfectly coordinated with the car's interior color.

Sue's presence in the passenger seat was also quite striking, with her long brown ponytail. Brent thought he met her for the first time at a summer dance as she was entering high school, one year behind him. But, in fact, they played together as young kids on her family farm when he and L.J. made visits to romp around the fields and woodlands with her older brother, Paul. Something about her apparently changed during her last year in middle school, unaware to Brent as he started high school in a separate building that year. Or maybe it was the live band playing their favorite songs, or her white shorts and summer tan. Regardless, this circling back to an acquaintance made in childhood instilled lasting impressions. As one result, Duke rode in the back seat of the car whenever Sue was around.

Another change came about during this time. Brent's friends began referring to him as "Sam"—his first name. His parents continued calling him by his middle name, Brent, to avoid confusion with his father, Sam. There was no definitive reason for his friends adopting this change. "Sam" could have been more fitting for someone participating in sports, or maybe it just sounded better when paired with "Sue." (Hopefully this does not cause any confusion as this story progresses.) So, Sam's F-85 Cutlass served him well for at least six months until the front ball joints deteriorated to where the front wheels could no longer roll in a vertical position. Sam, Sue, and Duke were then restricted to driving the town only when older Sam allowed the use of his vehicle.

The automobile represents one of man's wheel-related inventions—a system of circles starting with a cycling of pistons and an assortment of sprockets and gears, all connected to rotate the drive shaft and turn the wheel axles. Talk about impact. This invention not only put "America on wheels," but it completely transformed the world, immensely accelerating the Industrial Revolution. Unfortunately, the circular system powering this machine does not provide a way for carbon, a component of its fuel that is extracted from the ground, to return to the earth. Instead, as gasoline combusts, carbon spews into the atmosphere as a waste product in the form of carbon dioxide (CO_2) and traps heat, which is now known to be causing global warming and resulting in worldwide climate change. Scientists are warning that if this continues, droughts will become more severe, and rainstorms having greater intensity will become more frequent, causing increased flooding. Worse yet, as the polar ice caps melt, sea levels will rise, putting many coastal cities underwater.

Prior to the automobile and the Industrial Revolution in general, the world benefited from a "carbon cycle," or budget, that balanced the amount of CO_2 in the atmosphere by transferring it back and forth between plants and animals and burying excess carbon. It starts with photosynthesis. Green plants use this process to make food from CO_2, water, and sunlight. The process breaks CO_2 apart, trapping carbon within plants as they grow larger, while expelling oxygen into the atmosphere. People and critters use the oxygen by combining it with their ingested plant-based food (plants or animals that eat plants) to fuel their life-sustaining activities like movement and digestion. This process, known as respiration, "oxidizes" food. It's a chemical reaction that reattaches oxygen from the air to carbon from food. As this happens, energy is released into animals' bodies allowing

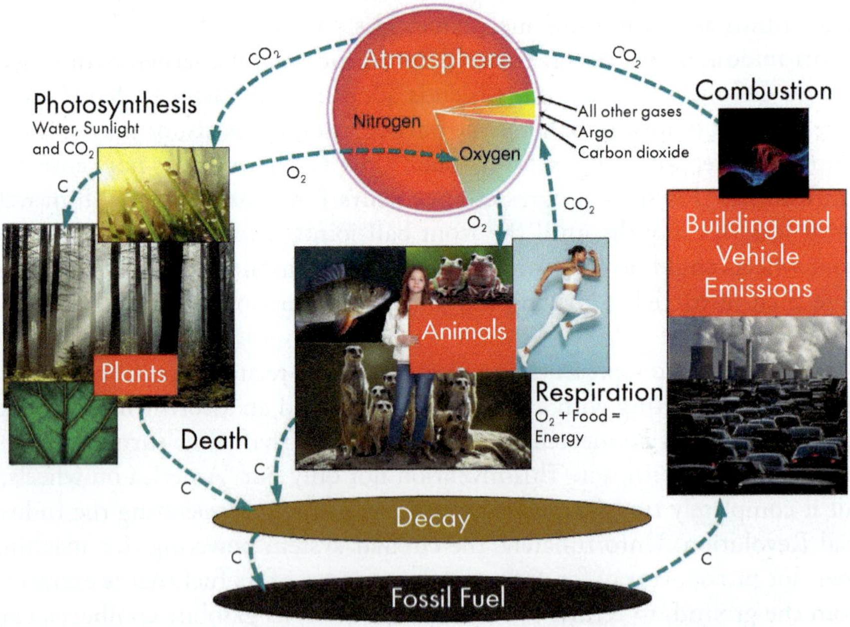

Figure 10.1. The carbon cycle with industrial age carbon added to the budget.

them to function. The new CO_2 is outbreathed as a waste product into the atmosphere where it can return to the plant world. As plants and animals die, carbon stored in their biomass neatly becomes part of the earth. What a plan! Who woulda thunk it? It's amazing how this carbon trade between plants and animals safely maintained itself in balance for millions of years.

So, why are we witnessing a sudden disruption of this balance in the past couple decades? In reality, the disruption began about 200 years ago, which is still a relatively short time—only about three human lifespans. Actions taken during this time in clearing forests to feed the Industrial Revolution and destroying wetlands to provide space for widespread urbanization appeared to be minimal. However, incremental changes, which went almost unnoticed, gradually combined to obliterate much of earth's plant world. Meanwhile, new homes, factories, cars, and people multiplied immensely, sparking increased mining and combustion of fossil fuels, which triggered the release of more CO_2. The flood of CO_2 into the atmosphere with fewer green plants to manage the carbon trade has increasingly pushed the needle since the early 1800s.

Prior to the Industrial Revolution, excess carbon resulting from dead and decaying plants and animals was compressed below earth's surface to become fossil fuel and remained untouched for millions of years. Today this stored carbon is being pumped back into the air at an incredible rate by cars, trucks, lawn mowers, leaf blowers, chain saws, motorboats, homes, factories, and buildings of all kinds, simultaneously, and with a dwindling plant population to recapture it. Since the middle of the 20th century, annual emissions from burning fossil fuels have increased every decade. In 2013, CO_2 levels overreached their highest levels in recorded history. This recent rise in CO_2 runs parallel with the history of fossil fuel burning and is accounted for based on knowing that about 60% of fossil fuel emissions stay in the air.

As CO_2 emissions increased, plant life diminished. Over the past 80 years, just one lifetime, many woodlands that survived Michigan's lumbering era were replaced by the needs and wants of baby boomers, with most forest removals happening during the first half of this period. This was the story in the greater Mud Lake area, as new subdivisions were constructed in the 1950s followed by new schools, shopping centers, and other developments to service the population increase. Natural area destruction in southeast Michigan was even greater, compounded by white flight from Detroit, where thousands of families left the city for new homes in surrounding greenfield suburbs. The automobile combined with superhigh-

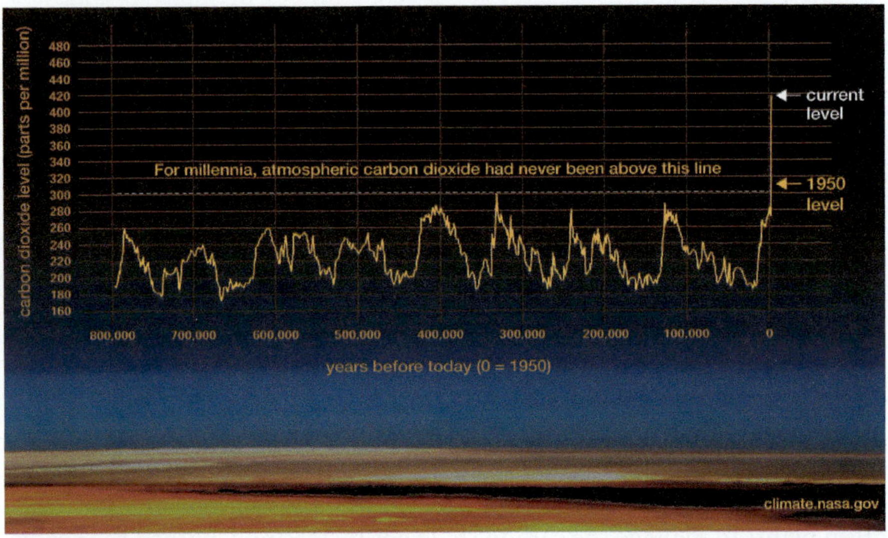

Figure 10.2. After staying in check for thousands of years, levels of carbon dioxide in the atmosphere appear to have skyrocketed shortly after the Industrial Revolution began. Image credit: Luthi, D., et al. 2008; Etheridge, D.M., et al. 2010; Vostok ice core data/J.R. Petit et al.; NOAA Mauna Loa CO2 record.

ways allowed this to happen, further worsening the CO_2 emission problem as people began commuting longer distances. This is beginning to sound like a vicious circle!

References

10.2: Composition of the Atmosphere, in Earth Science 10.2.1 (CK-12 Foundation 2023), *available at* https://k12.libretexts.org/Bookshelves/Science_and_Technology/Earth_Science/10%3A_Atmospheric_Processes/10.02%3A_Composition_of_the_Atmosphere.

Conversations and E-mail Correspondence With Becky Goodman, Downtown Director, City of Petoskey (Feb. 22 - Apr. 28, 2022).

National Aeronautics and Space Administration (NASA) Global Climate Change, *Graphic: The Relentless Rise of Carbon Dioxide*, https://climate.nasa.gov/climate_resources/24/graphic-the-relentless-rise-of-carbon-dioxide/ (last updated May 25, 2023).

NASA Global Climate Change, *The Causes of Climate Change*, https://climate.nasa.gov/causes/ (last updated May 25, 2023).

Chapter 11
Racial Injustice and Mud Lake

Winter fishing on Mud Lake continued but less frequently throughout Sam's high school days and even more seldom once in college. Sue became his most regular fishing buddy, particularly after they married. She grew up in a fishing household and found the sport quite enjoyable, providing someone baited her hook and dehooked her fish. Once home or to Sam and Marilyn's house to share the catch, she had no desire to see the fish until they were cleaned and ready for the fry pan. She then displayed one of her true talents—frying fish. Her way and her father-in-law's way had some differences, although both were great, which always sparked up fun discussion.

Sue grew up several miles outside of the greater Mud Lake area on a farm with six siblings. Like Becky, she was responsible for her brother, two years younger. But with no next-door friend to distract her attention, she was more focused on her brother's activities, to the point of making him a full-time pal. Their outdoor adventures held resemblances to those of the Mud Lake kids. It was just a different woods, marsh, and pond. However, being the appointed kid in charge, her guiding persona became ingrained at an early age, which served her and Sam well, especially as she assumed motherhood.

By the time they hitched, word had circulated about the good fishing at Mud Lake, and on nice days, small crowds would gather on the ice with some folks coming from out of town. One winter near the end of January, the most peculiar trio arrives, dragging a small canoe loaded with all their fishing gear. Not knowing where the hot spots might be, they pull their canoe near a group of other fishermen. They make three holes in the ice, drop in their baited lines, and take their seats inside the canoe. A short distance away, the other fishermen notice the trio to be of Asian descent, which was nonexistent in their hometown, as was their style of fishing. They avoid conversation with the trio, other than a few disparaging remarks followed by group chuckling. With the fishing a little slow that day, only a short time passes before the threesome packs up and leaves the lake.

In addition to environmentalism, the issue of racism was overshadowed as the Vietnam War raged during the 1960s. Riots burned out, and demonstrations lost their gas. With some apparent positive advancements on racial issues following Dr. Martin Luther King's death, people seemed to accept the status quo, and most chose to talk about other things. Yet a silent favoring of white supremacy still lingered in the minds of many—in some without consciously knowing it. This destructive movement would continue smoldering until late in the second decade of the next century, when, with the rise of Donald Trump, a new acceptance of white supremacy was unleashed among those sharing this view.

The racial event that occurred on Mud Lake in the early 1970s, close to Dr. King's birthday, did not seem terrible during that time. Imagine a throwback of 1950 mindsets experiencing a TV commercial produced in 2022. Seeing the level of diversity displayed in these advertisements would certainly trigger some derogatory commentary. Yet today, these ads employing people of all races interacting together while consuming everyday products are accepted as standard procedure. This is life in America—or at least on American TV.

On a more intense level, when European settlers could not accept the ways of our nation's indigenous people, they were not just ridiculed, they were removed, which apparently seemed acceptable at that time. The truth about what happened remained concealed for more than a century, as young boys of the 1950s role-played as cowboys and Indians with no clue about the unjust slaughter of Native Americans. The wrongness of this atrocity was not openly discussed until late in the 1900s, suggesting that adults in the '50s knew it was wrong but would rather sweep it under the rug than speak out about the truth. Somehow or other, the social perception of right and wrong and the degree of each got mixed up in the time continuum.

Prejudice against Blacks surfaced in the neighborhood near Mud Lake during the same time local fishermen shunned the Chinese trio. This was when Rod and LaVerne started having serious concerns about race issues and undergoing long discussions about liberty, love, race, and religion after putting their kids to bed. Realizing the Haslett community had no people of color, they connected with the American Civil Liberties Union (ACLU) and National Association for the Advancement of Colored People (NAACP) to assist in circulating open housing petitions in local neighborhoods. Going door-to-door, some signed the petition, some were afraid, and some just said no.

A few weeks later, one Sunday afternoon, an African-American couple with their kids came to see a house for sale about a half block up the road from the Hagenbuchs' place. Their little boy borrowed one of the resident kids' bikes to ride a short distance down the road and back. Shortly after the house shoppers left, neighbors began gathering in the street. A loud-talking man leading the discussion appeared to have been imbibing a bit before getting the group together. Following some harsh discussion and pointing at the house for sale, they all went into the loud man's house.

LaVerne is out the door like a shot, walks up the street, and knocks on the door to enter. After about a half hour she returns home smiling. Without revealing a lot of details, she simply tells Rod she asked a couple of questions and had a nice chat with the loud man in front of the group. She thanked them for letting her join the conversation, and that was it. Rod smiled knowing what the poor jerk went through, having tried to argue unsupportable positions with her himself. In civil arguments, she was totally destructive by pure logic, without using harsh words or a loud voice. That was the last that Rod and LaVerne heard about race and housing in the neighborhood. Several years later, Beth acquired an adopted, biracial, younger sister, Patty, one of the first children of color in Haslett schools.

As we continue to sort out what happened with African Americans over the past 400 years and recognize their contributions to our American heritage, our understanding about the meaning of equality is getting clearer. Education about truthful African-American history will further enhance this clarity. Dr. King summed it up well when he said, "It really boils down to this: that all life is interrelated. We are all caught in an inescapable network of mutuality, tied into a single garment of destiny." Could this be something to do with our connection to the movement of larger objects or, more simply, the movement of time itself?

Dr. King initially focused his work on the inalienable human rights of Black people in white America, but his work also included fights against poverty and the Vietnam War, and more, as he said in a letter from a Birmingham jail, "Injustice anywhere is a threat to justice everywhere. . . . Whatever affects one directly, affects all indirectly." The connection between King's faith and his work for justice or between spirituality and service to the world for the common good can be found not only in his life but in the lives of many people who see themselves as spiritual (or religious).

The idea of spirituality, which is strongly rooted in the greater Mud Lake area, is widespread among Americans, yet somewhat undefined. The Fetzer Institute in Kalamazoo, Michigan, conducted a "Study of Spirituality in the United States" and reported that most people consider themselves spiritual to some extent and say that spirituality is important in their lives. In addition, spirituality relates to an engaged civic life: people who identify as highly spiritual are more likely to say it is important to make a difference in their communities and to contribute to greater good in the world.

While the study's key findings highlight the importance of "a strong sense of connection to humanity," its results also show a connection to nature is very important. The report identifies a connection to nature as one of the consistent themes coming from focus group discussions. In fact, two-thirds of the focus group participants said they were "touched by the beauty of creation." Within the groups, people of all spiritual and religious identifications, and even those who said they were not spiritual, described specific experiences—recently or long ago—of peace, awe, mystery, or wonder in the natural world. One response, for example;

> Every time I see a certain animal, like a butterfly, that's a really small spiritual experience. Because to me, they're just so interesting how they have short lives, but their whole lives are spent with a purpose for making sure their species stays alive.
>
> *Amanda, 21*
> Moderately spiritual/Not religious at all

Is it possible that ancient stories written by people in various locations of the world as guiding principles for behavior are becoming outdated? All being quite similar, these books served their purpose well among their regional, religious followers. Yet due to subtle differences, they have inspired disagreement, hate, immense pain, and death for millions when aggression is cast against another group's doctrine. For similar reasons but scaled down a bit, the Mud Lake locals took offense against the visual differences portrayed by the Asian trio and Black house shoppers. How amazing it would be if knowledge and truth about the natural world baked with love, which seems to be universally important, could be distilled and embraced by everyone as the underlying theme for living, without getting hung up on regional-specific or tribal details.

Caution: Thinking about this too long may be hazardous to your health. Although according to Rachel Carson, maybe not.

References

Telephone Interviews and E-mail Correspondence With Bridget Booth, Certified Environmental Educator, Science Teacher at Haslett Middle School (Mar. 2 - Apr. 22, 2022).

Fetzer Institute, *What Does Spirituality Mean to Us?—Experiences*, https://spiritualitystudy.fetzer.org/key-findings/experiences (last visited May 31, 2023) ("Two in three people frequently feel touched by the beauty of creation.").

Stephanie Gagnon, *"All Life Is Interrelated": Dr. Martin Luther King Jr.'s Environmental Justice Legacy*, NWF Blog (Oct. 24, 2022), https://blog.nwf.org/2019/01/all-life-is-interrelated-dr-martin-luther-king-jr-s-environmental-justice-legacy/.

Telephone Interviews and E-mail Correspondence With Beth Hagenbuch, Landscape Architect (Feb. 11 - Apr. 5, 2022).

Rodney Hagenbuch, Rodney Hagenbuch Memoir (1965) (unpublished manuscript).

Martin Luther King Jr., *"Injustice Anywhere Is a Threat to Justice Everywhere . . .,"* Dayton Daily News (Jan. 19, 2014), https://www.daytondailynews.com/news/opinion/injustice-anywhere-threat-justice-everywhere/6kof5N2GN7CZmrILgOlSxK/.

Conversations With Susan Lovall, Grandmother and Mud Lake Enthusiast (Nov. 2021-Dec. 2022).

Chapter 12
Mud Lake's Family Circle

The Detroit River

Figure 12.1. Map showing approximate locations of wetlands in the Detroit River 200 years ago compared to today (conceptual diagram with information taken from several non-conforming sources).

Michigan's first attraction to European settlers happened along the Detroit River flanked by rich coastal wetlands teaming with fish and wildlife. One of the first arrivals, Antoine de la Mothe Cadillac noted, "The area is so temperate, so fertile, and so beautiful that it may justly be called the earthly paradise of North America." In Cadillac's time, coastal wetlands lined the 32-mile-long river on both sides, in some areas up to a mile wide. Unfortunately, more than 99% of these wetlands along the Michigan side no longer exist due to shoreline filling and hardening. Understanding how coastal wetlands provide recreational opportunities, floodwater protection, water filtering, and carbon storage, along with harboring fish and wildlife—an important food source—environmental leaders of this region are diligently working to stop wetland destruction and to recreate them.

The economy of southeast Michigan once thrived on fish and wildlife resources. After these resources provided sustenance to indigenous peoples for thousands of years, early European settlers exploited the lands and waters for profit. They slaughtered nearly all the lake sturgeon and drove the beaver population to near extinction by taking their hides for the sale of fur hats. With beavers just about gone and the Industrial Revolution heating up, moneymaking transitioned to shipbuilding, steelmaking, and automobile manufacturing—all making use of rivers and the Great Lakes to operate. And now, with the trending, new "blue economy," renewed importance is placed on clean water along with healthy fish and wildlife to support outdoor recreation. After doing almost everything possible to exploit and destroy fish and wildlife habitat, people have come full circle—needing the environment to be in good condition for our new economy to prosper!

Revitalization work at the Ford Rouge Center includes a "living roof" growing on top of the Dearborn Truck Plant. Planted with a drought-tolerant groundcover called sedum, the living roof is one of the world's largest, spanning 10.4 acres. The plants slow down and filter storm water runoff while trapping airborne dust and absorbing carbon dioxide—providing ecosystem services much like wetlands. The roof also offers habitat for birds and pollinating insects.

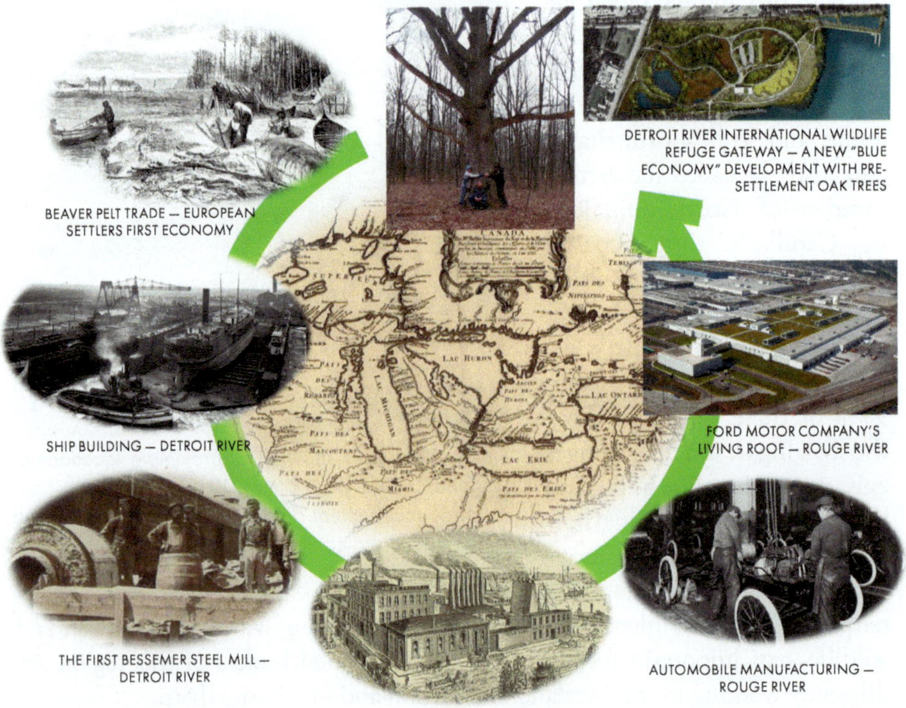

Figure 12.2. Southeast Michigan's transitioning economy comes full circle—returning to a need for clean waterways while continuing to revolve around the Great Lakes.

Images from the Wisconsin Historical Society (center image), Library of Congress (Beaver Pelt Trade & Ship Building), Collections of The Wyandotte Museums (First Bessemer Steel Mill) (cropped from original), Collections of The Henry Ford (Machine Shops & Automobile Manufacturing), Roy Feldman and McDonough + Partners (Ford Motor Living Roof), USFWS & Hamilton Anderson Associates (Detroit River), and John H. Hartig (oak tree).

A former DiamlerChrysler paint factory site was transformed into the visitor gateway for the Detroit River International Wildlife Refuge. Situated near the Humbug Marsh, which is the last remaining mile of historic coastal wetland on the U.S. side of the Detroit River, this site is now a hub for outdoor recreation including fishing, birding, hunting, kayaking, and wildlife observation. It is interesting to see some of the trees that sprouted as saplings during the first European settlers' "beaver economy" are still standing as we continue our reliance on water resources.

Lake Lansing (Pine Lake)

Economic phasing in the Mud Lake area evolved in a similar circular pattern, revolving around the area's natural water resources. Native Americans harvested fish and wildlife riches in and around Pine Lake while working nearby fertile soils for crops. The area evolved into a transportation center with trails heading several directions to similar places having life-sustaining resources.

European settlers robbed indigenous peoples of their assets in the early 1800s; however, the area's agrarian economy continued with only cultural differences, leaving Native Americans worse for it. As the white population increased, so did revenue from agriculture. With the arrival of a pass-through railroad, the region became more accessible, attracting Michigan spiritualists to the natural beauty near Pine Lake. This same attraction fueled the development of an entertainment destination, complete with a wild amusement park, serving nearby cities. Unfortunately, like similar destinations during that time, thrill-producing attractions proved to be unsustainable, and they eventually faded into the history books.

Today, with the transportation infrastructure connecting to stable workplaces like Michigan State University in East Lansing and state capitol offices in downtown Lansing, the Haslett community continues its reliance on the lake to attract and brand its market along with establishing its identity of place. This is typified by the amusement park's redevelopment into a clean "beach park" hosting simple things like a bathhouse, multipurpose dock, summer snack bar, playground, and picnic grounds with shelters. The historic carousel building is preserved as a reminder of the park's rich history. Next to the park, locals and visitors patronize the Blue Gill Grill and the Mayfair, Ingham County's oldest neighborhood bar, both complete with rooftop seating to enjoy views to the lake. Natural resources clearly remain the area's economic driver, and their cleanliness is essential to enhance businesses and attract new residents.

Figure 12.3. Economic phasing in the Mud Lake area evolved in a circular pattern, revolving around the area's natural resources.

Images courtesy of the Library of Congress (Fishing & Hunting), © Lansing State Journal-USA TODAY NETWORK (Amusement Park), and The Mayfair Bar (Izzer Entertainment Club & Mayfair Rooftop).

People in the greater Mud Lake area understood the importance of preserving the valuable water resources offered by Lake Lansing when first encountering its benefits long before good stewardship practices were known. In the early days, they just did things that seemed appropriate without thoroughly understanding what might be causing a problem or if any negative impacts would result from their actions. To remedy the lake's weed problem in 1907, they constructed a dam across the outlet, raising the lake water level by approximately three feet. Various fish-stocking efforts were made between 1920 and 1990 that included an assortment of panfish along with walleye, tiger muskellunge, and channel catfish. In July 1922, the *Lansing State Journal* published an article regarding the weed problems in Pine Lake with the headline "Plan to Rid Pine Lake of Weed Crop—Lake Will Be Solid Weed Bed Unless Action Is Taken This Season." The article described a citizen-fabricated program to destroy the weeds, which unfortunately yielded little success.

Studies between 1938 and 1941 showed dissolved oxygen content was zero at a depth of 21 feet, and the muddy bottom was loaded with emergent and submergent aquatic plants. One report stated that the overdeveloped lake had 130 cottages, two resorts, and four boat liveries with even more cottage development occurring along the east shore. However, the lake's brown coloring flawed the reputation of these developments.

Fortunately, being near the state capitol and the only inland lake having potential for high recreational value in mid-Michigan, Lake Lansing received some extra attention. So, monitoring continued. In 1950, Allan Tucker, who went on to establish the Institute for Academic Leadership at Florida State University, authored a report about the regular occurrence of phytoplankton with reference to phosphorus. Water chemistry samples were collected from Lake Lansing as a basis for his research, which was sponsored by Michigan State University. Total phosphorus values on all sampling dates ranged from 13 to 17 micrograms per liter except for the deepest water samples, which were 33 and 57 micrograms per liter—all very high. This study identified phosphorus, which was leaching into the lake from leaky septic tanks, adjacent fertilized lawns, and nearby farm fields, to be causing the weed problem.

In 1955, some area residents started an aquatic plant-cutting operation to remove unwanted plants from the lake, but it did not continue for long due to public controversy. Two years later, the Michigan Department of Conservation began a sodium arsenite treatment to control aquatic plants in the lake. Data collected during this time showed plants to be less abundant, but so were the fish! A mortality of approximately 5,000 fish occurred in June 1959. In one report, the reduction of dissolved oxygen levels was thought to have caused the mortality. However, a conflicting memo from the Michigan Water Resources Commission attributed the cause to a spraying of DDT on uplands near the lake. A second fish kill of about 5,000 was observed in 1963 with no cause identified.

In the early 1960s, a sanitary sewer was constructed around Lake Lansing to eliminate nutrient enrichment by individual septic systems. Following this huge improvement, Lake Lansing became a petri dish for study by professional firms and public institutions, with reports published almost every year for the next three decades. A flurry of study led up to 1978, when between then and 1983 approximately 1.6 million cubic yards of soft sediment were dredged from the lake and 220,890 cubic yards of sand were redistributed to restore the lake bottom. More study followed regarding the restoration project's results. Brief summaries of these can be found online in Appendix A of the *Management Plan for Lake Lansing and Its Watershed* prepared by Progressive AE in 2002.

Lake Lansing's management plan mentions some of the earlier issues that were addressed by state and county agencies, such as the influences of the former "dump" on the southeast shore; the levels of arsenic in lake sediments and groundwater; the use of waste oil for dust control on nearby Mallard Street; high bacterial levels in the beach area; poor fishing quality; and abundant nuisance aquatic plants. More recently, recreational use pressure and the introduction and spread of exotic plant and animal species are identified as issues of concern. Eurasian water milfoil and curly-leaf pondweed are the most problematic aquatic invasive plants, while fertilized lawns backing up seawalls pose an even greater threat. These need replacement by native shoreline emergent plants as a first step to control the invasive aquatics.

Historical water quality and aquatic plant data suggest that Lake Lansing has been eutrophic for quite some time. After Lake Lansing was dredged in 1978, some improvement in water quality was reported. However, the dredging project along with increased development in the area probably increased recreational pressure as well, as was predicted in early studies.

With guidance by a special Lake Lansing Advisory Committee over a five-year period, the water management plan project team conducted water quality monitoring, nuisance exotic plant control, and engaged interested citizens to obtain input on goals and strategies for future management efforts. Findings noted that Lake Lansing is generally in good health, and the water quality is generally good. Other remarks included the following partial list:

- Historical records indicate that, for many years, the lake has been and continues to be eutrophic (i.e., nutrient-enriched and biologically productive). Phosphorus is noted as the primary nutrient of concern, since one pound of phosphorus can generate 500 pounds of aquatic plants.
- Ambient total phosphorus concentrations in the lake are high enough to stimulate excessive plant growth.
- The largest controllable sources of phosphorus appear to be rain runoff from residential and urban areas, including that transported to the lake via storm drains.
- During peak boating times, Lake Lansing is severely overcrowded. During periods of more typical use, the lake is at its threshold for sus-

taining safe boating. Any additional boating pressure, either from the county park or from keyhole lots, could compromise safety.

- Lake Lansing-area residents identified two major goals in their desire to manage the lake:

  1. Maintain and improve the environmental quality of Lake Lansing and its watershed.
  2. Maintain and improve recreational opportunities and public safety in Lake Lansing and its watershed.

- There are five geographic areas within the Lake Lansing watershed that are critical for water quality improvement and protection:

  1. Storm drainage systems
  2. Riparian residential lands
  3. Other residential lands within the watershed
  4. Wetlands
  5. Undeveloped lands

From a comprehensive list of recommendations, a few are noted here:

- Continue management of aquatic plant growth.
- Continue lake water quality monitoring.
- Continue disseminating riparian and watershed education/information to homeowners, as well as lake users through the Ingham County Park System.
- Make physical improvements to lake-area storm drains.
- Install wetland filters to trap pollutants.
- Establish special "lake area" zoning for redevelopment purposes.
- Make wetland purchases and establish conservation easements.
- Install riparian vegetative buffers.
- Implement natural roadside planting.
- Develop alternative funding methods, possibly grants, to pay for the larger, more permanent structural projects.
- Reduce phosphorus and contaminant loading from the watershed area.

The restoration and preservation of Lake Lansing's precious water resources clearly was and remains a public priority. With much of this effort happening during the 1960s and '70s, somewhat under the radar, Lake Lansing's health is considerably better for it. In looking back, it is apparent that many of Lake Lansing's problems came about from too much love. In contrast, Mud Lake received almost no attention—no studies, no maintenance recommendations, and no actions to protect or restore its water quality until Haslett Public Schools purchased the property. And then it only included some water sampling by biology teachers to add substance to their students' classwork. Even though the lake and surrounding wetland served as a powerhouse in filtering water before entering the underlying aquifer, and it provided a wonderland for children's adventures, its eutrophication process went unnoticed.

Homelife for kids around Lake Lansing during these times was different but, in many ways, the same as near Mud Lake. It is all one community. The Sack family lived in the neighborhood just southeast of Lake Lansing, not far from Haslett Road. This was the older part of town wedged between the retail/bar/restaurant district near the lake and more retail mixed with older residences along Haslett Road. Unlike in the new subdivisions, most street trees were fully grown. It had a town-like feel but not at all uppity. The tree canopy included a wide mix of shade trees including volunteer specimens. A giant mulberry tree in front of the library covered the sidewalk with purple stain every summer along with every kids' fingers and lips in town. Where sidewalks existed, they were in disrepair, as were some of the houses, which varied from dilapidated summer cottages to substantial two-story, early 20th century homes. Backyard gardens were common, which supported statements of pride and vegetable trading among neighbors. Yet these patches of green were simply seen as snack bars by kids who ran the neighborhood.

The Sacks' two boys, Rick and Terry, showed above-average scholastic and athletic ability—attributes of notice in any small town. Their father worked as a mailman, so he knew some details about where other kids lived—both good and bad, and he watched closely over his boys. Terry was introduced to the youngsters growing up around Mud Lake in early elementary school, but the group separated in fourth grade when Wilkshire Elementary opened, and many of the kids living in Lakeview Heights were assigned to the new school. However, they all rejoined in junior high and became close friends, with bicycles eliminating the distance barrier.

Terry's early engagement with the natural world centered around Lake Lansing. The weed-infested south end had features similar to Mud Lake, like soft edges bordered by marshland. This swampy zone, briefly interrupted by

East Lake Drive, followed the railroad tracks to Okemos-Haslett Road (later to become Marsh Road) and well beyond, making a haven for catching frogs, snakes, and turtles.

A northeasterly trip on Lake Drive led to "the Dump"—a mini landfill in the wetland that eventually provided high enough ground to stage a recycling center. Here is where everyone in town unloaded unwanted things that they couldn't burn in their backyard, prior to any thoughts about recycling. Trips to the Dump were typically handled by dads and their kids. The winding road through the swamp bellowed with frog talk and presented surprises like being stopped by a heavyweight snapping turtle thinking he owned the road and needing a prod with a long stick to keep cars moving. When arriving at the Dump, a familiar stench streamed into the open car windows, and a man with a hook replacing one of his hands greeted the dumpers. After a quick scan over the load, he gave directions for where to dump the stuff, sometimes requesting certain items be set near his small shelter. The area was clearly signed in several locations, "No Picking." So, dads had plenty of justification for saying "no" to youngsters who wanted to root through the piles of cans, jars, and other rubbish.

For Terry, the lake's north end held more appealing natural attractions. Although the water quality wasn't great, a sandy beach at the Dells Nightclub lakefront was one of only a few good swimming places in the entire Lansing area. Kids would come here by the carload from no telling where. Nearby, the Pine Lake Outlet offered another adventure opportunity. Fishing near the outlet with marshmallow bits for bait could bring in a few bluegills, and hiking down the outlet through the marsh was comparable to swamp stomping in First Creek. When needing a dangerous challenge, climbing the billboard on Marsh Road substituted for a water tower ascent and made a strategic place to launch tomatoes.

By sixth grade, Terry's family moved out of the lake neighborhood to a new ranch home on Marsh Road, across the street from the Shaw family—a longtime Haslett clan with two cheerleading daughters and a younger son. With all Haslett kids now combined into one junior high building, Terry's relationship with Lakeview Heights kids grew even tighter from his new living location on the subdivision's westerly edge. However, bicycle adventures carried the guys well beyond the town area to places like the Park Lake Road gravel pits, near the edge of East Lansing. This chain of deep spring-fed swimming holes, surrounded by forest, offered a secluded oasis for older-kid play that continued into their high school years. Nighttime travel on bikes was common as well. Meeting up in the Shoptown Plaza parking lot until well after dark on hot summer nights was a regular occurrence, as was sleeping out-of-doors, which completely eliminated the idea of a curfew.

During one group outdoor sleeping event, the boys made a trip to visit the neighborhood girls who were grouped up on the upper floor of Lois Martin's garage. No one knew what might happen, but there was potential for some kissing, since a few crushes sparked between the two groups.

The guys arrived a little before midnight and quietly parked their bikes behind the garage with care not to wake Lois' parents. Navigating by moonlight made finding the door on the building's opposite side challenging. Once in, it was single file up the stairs. In their diligence to keep quiet, every creaking step sounded like an electrically amplified, out-of-tune violin. Upon reaching the upper wood-planked floor, they find the girls tucked in their sleeping bags wielding flashlights and doing their best to hold back the giggles. The guys stumble into places to sit, and the chatter begins. With the noise level rising, Lois anxiously whispers a warning, "Keep your voices down, or my dad will be out here!" This worked for a while, and someone might have been kissed, but the chatter and giggling eventually gets out of control. This puts Lois over the edge, and she calls it to an end—the boys had to leave. Everyone understands, so without argument, just more giggling, the guys make their way back to the stairs, where Terry accidentally catches his toe on a galvanized bucket and nudges it, bouncing to the lower level. What a racket! Kicking that bucket slaughters any attempt to be silent. The girls' giggling erupts to screaming laughter as the boys stampede down the stairs, fearing they are sure to be caught by Mr. Martin. Laughing out of fright, they make it back to their bikes and zoom into the darkness—back to their own sleeping bags. Fortunately, Lois' parents were deep sleepers, and the girls never saw Mr. Martin that night. But Terry never heard the end of how he "kicked the bucket," killing the night's silence.

This event marked the beginning of a decade or more of sorting between the two genders to determine who would pair together to foster the next generation of kids. Millions of telephone conversations, movie dates, dances, picnics, beach trips, ice cream cones, zoo visits, and songs on the radio served as venues to test relationships in the sorting process.

Aside from the recreational treasures around Lake Lansing and areawide bicycle travels during Terry's junior high years, the Lake Lansing Amusement Park ranked high on his fun list. It was revered as the premier amusement park in mid-Michigan in its early days. This rare gem handed down from a previous generation etched exceptional memories into the heads of Lansing-area kids during the 1950s and '60s, but only a few could say the park was almost in their backyard. The thunderous Cyclone roller coaster could be heard from anywhere in town. But from Terry's lake-neighborhood house, it clanked up its track and crashed down in stereo with the buzz of a wild "bug" ride at the other end of the park and all the voices of laughter and thrill in between. Regular trips to the park were both fun and educational. This is where Terry and most Haslett kids learned to drive—both on the Turnpike and the Dodgem!

Figure 12.4. Gas powered cruisers under total control of their drivers zoomed round the Turnpike track–a grown-up experience for 8th graders and their dates.
Image credit: © Bill Duchaine–USA TODAY NETWORK.

Figure 12.5. Loud scrapping and sparking on the ceiling by the electric power rods attached to each car made the bumping and crashing a secondary thrill.
Image credit: © Bill Duchaine–USA TODAY NETWORK

Special days at the park like the Fourth of July unleashed even more fun. Afternoon hot-air balloon ascensions were popular attractions. After drifting high over the lake, the balloonist would abandon his craft with a parachute to the water, leaving the balloon to wander out of control to wherever it might land. A chase squad usually found it near the Pines or as far as Green Road. Spectacular fireworks displayed over the water ended the day for parkgoers and most everyone in town, who were enjoying the evening out-of-doors.

Even though the park seemed like an eternal place for fun, its days were numbered. Dwindling attendance in the 1960s and increasing maintenance costs took their toll. During this time, the roller coaster occasionally shut down due to safety concerns. It always looked rickety, adding to its mystique, but now the existence of real danger loomed in the minds of potential riders. All the attractions were acquiring an aged appearance, and fires eventually ravaged the park, leading to its ultimate end.

The first fire took out most of the midway games including the shooting gallery, milk bottle toss, and floating duck grab. Worse yet, the fun-in-the-dark ride was lost. This thrilling car ride carried those who dared through pitch-dark rooms with slamming doors and neck-jerking sharp turns, accompanied by startling noises and unexpected flashes of scary stuff. Skee-Ball was the only salvaged attraction in this strip after the fire—a serious wound to the park.

With evening visitors becoming a bit rowdy, the admission price was increased to cut out the riffraff. It may have sorted out some troublemakers, but family visitation continued to decline, only furthering the problem of sparse crowds. The Casino, which held a prominent waterfront position, was known to Terry and other young '60s kids as a roller-skating rink, giving a place to burn off energy every weekend throughout the winter. But a decision was made to transition the skating rink into an arcade by moving coin-operated gaming machines, previously used in the park's midway, onto the rink floor. Beautiful antique pinball machines in fine wood cases filled the great room where a giant glass chandelier ball previously twirled above music-driven skaters. The games were nice, but after a few visits, they didn't entertain the kids as well as the kids could entertain each other while skating. Eventually the machines were again moved into storage areas making way for rock concerts—the perfect venue for amusement park-loving kids that grew into teenagers looking for a change. In 1968, Terry organized his friends to buy tickets for a show featuring Bob Seger, Brownsville Station,

Figure 12.6. The Casino occupied a prominent position on the shoreline and housed a variety of attractions.
Image credit: Pauline Sprague

and the MC5 (Motor City 5). If harnessed, the energy that night could have ran every ride in the park.

After several efforts to revive the park, revenues could no longer sustain its existence, so in the early 1970s, the owner, Roland Johnson, began selling his assets. Salvageable rides were offered to any potential takers and the land eventually went to Ingham County for a future park development. The park's historic Dentzel carousel, which was added in 1942 and remained until 1971, was dismantled and sold to Cedar Point for use in its Frontier Land. The train that went under the coaster and around the park was sold to David Aldrich, who ran the food concessions in Lansing's Potter Park Zoo. Aldrich operated the train there until 1985, when a train ride accident occurred at the Detroit Zoo, raising all ride-operator insurance rates around the state and eliminating any profit in the train ticket price.

Aldrich and one of his Haslett-area friends also negotiated a deal with Johnson to purchase the arcade along with all its contents for $1,200. In the first weekend after the sale, they spent some enjoyable time looking over their new stuff and moved 12 pinball machines into off-site garages with the idea of beginning a major move the next weekend. But during that next week, the Casino/arcade building caught fire and burnt to the ground. Unfortunately, there was no insurance. Results of the investigation concluded that a homeless person had apparently broken in, built a fire in a bathtub to keep warm, and lost control of it. All was lost.

Finally, in 1973, Lake Lansing Amusement Park closed except for the Cyclone, which was demolished the following year. Sam and Sue were married in '73 and moved into Pine Lake Apartments, just north of the park, a stone's throw from where Obed Marshall, the area's first European settler, built his log cabin 137 years prior. They soaked in as many coaster rides as they could that summer, knowing this blast from the past would soon be gone. The carousel building remains today to store lawn maintenance equipment for the county park as well as part of the track from the Turnpike ride, where kids now race tricycles for free.

Figure 12.7. The Cyclone roller coaster is the last ride removed from Lake Lansing Amusement Park in 1974.
Photo credit: *Lansing State Journal*, Dec. 11, 1974, p. 1.

Amusement parks around the state met a similar fate. These include Wenona Beach Park in Bay City (1887-1964), Ramona Park in East Grand Rapids (1897-1955), and Edgewater Park in Detroit (1927-1981), to name a few. Many served as recreational outlets during the "Golden Age"—the first 30 years of the 20th century. As this era's "Greatest Generation" began reaching maturity, and the amusement parks of their youth started looking old, new leisure-time activities gained popularity. Golf was a big one and remained a leading recreational pastime into the early 2000s. Michigan, like other parts of the country, experienced a course-building boom after World War II as young adults of the 1950s and their kids fully embraced the game. This construction frenzy was fueled by televised tournaments, golf industry enthusiasm, and developers who viewed courses as necessary amenities in residential projects.

Haslett received its version of golf as a nine-hole course known as Pine Lake Country Club. Located on the opposite side of the railroad tracks from the Dump, its proximity to Lake Lansing reinforced its namesake. Unfortunately, its placement and intensive use of fertilizer and pesticides necessary to maintain its lush lawns contradicted strategies that were later set forth in the lake's management plan to control phosphorus. We can only hope the wetland wrapping the lake's south end performed as it should in filtering out all the unwanted chemicals.

Mud Lake's Global Family

Interestingly, the Lake Lansing and Mud Lake watersheds receive drainage from land extending only several miles to the east, not far past Michigan's principal meridian. This north/south line, surveyed in 1815, roughly bisects the Lower Peninsula and was used as a reference line for all other survey work in the state. It was chosen because it formed one of the main boundary lines defined in the Treaty of Detroit in 1807, constituting the first large cession of Michigan Territory land by Native Americans to the United States. This land transfer defined by this imaginary line on the ground marked the beginning of a significant change to the mitten-shaped peninsula, which extends into the largest freshwater basin on earth, holding one-fifth of the world's aboveground freshwater supply. A couple decades later, in 1830 to be precise, the U.S. Congress passed the Indian Removal Act, which called for relocating all American Indians to lands west of the Mississippi River, leaving the Great Lakes region open to further development by European settlers. Michigan achieved statehood shortly thereafter (in 1837) and over the next 60 years, most forests, which had covered the penninsula, were cut down for farms and to produce lumber for buildings, ships, and mines.

The state's north/south ridgeline, which divides surface water flowing to Lake Michigan from water running easterly to Lake Huron and Lake Erie, is near the principal meridian. So, this ridge is also close to the eastern edge of the Lake Lansing and Mud Lake watersheds. Both lakes have outlets running westerly before joining together and merging with the Red Cedar River, which connects to the Grand River, ultimately emptying into Lake Michigan. In the big water, flow goes north, spiraling through the Straits of Mackinac, before heading back south through Lake Huron.

Like beginning a journey on the yellow brick road, headwaters from near this central Michigan ridgeline rest briefly in Mud Lake and Lake Lansing before wandering across the state and taking the long way around the peninsula to find the Detroit River, Lake Erie, and Lake Ontario, and then out the St. Lawrence Seaway. Prevailing westerly winds push the water across the Atlantic Ocean where it cycles through wetlands of Europe and Asia before returning across the Pacific and home to the Great Lakes Basin. Does the culturally historic and geographically prominent location of Lake Lansing and Mud Lake suggest this area is the beginning and ending of a large circle? Regardless, it is very apparent that multiple smaller circles began and ended in the Lake Lansing/Mud Lake area, with many still spinning.

References

From the Archives: Lake Lansing Amusement Park, LANSING STATE J. (Aug. 24, 2015), https://www.lansingstatejournal.com/story/news/local/2015/08/21/archives-lake-lansing-amusement-park/32142727/.

Telephone Interviews and E-mail Correspondence With Bridget Booth, Certified Environmental Educator, Science Teacher at Haslett Middle School (Mar. 2 - Apr. 22, 2022).

FRED DUSTIN, THE SAGINAW TREATY OF 1819 BETWEEN GENERAL LEWIS CASS AND THE CHIPPEWA INDIANS (1919), *available at* https://www.google.com/books/edition/The_Saginaw_Treaty_of_1819_Between_Gener/Wop0AAAAMAAJ.

John Hartig, *Great Lakes Moment: Rouge River Revived*, GREAT LAKES NOW (Oct. 7, 2022), https://www.greatlakesnow.org/2022/10/great-lakes-moment-rouge-river-revived/.

JOHN HARTIG, HONORING OUR DETROIT RIVER (2003).

Haslett/Lake Lansing Community Memories, *Tom Crawford Shared a Post*, FACEBOOK (Oct. 20, 2022), https://www.facebook.com/groups/265887632013194.

Ingham County Parks, *Lake Lansing Park South*, https://pk.ingham.org/parks/lake_lansing_south.php (last visited May 31, 2023).

Library of Archives Canada, *A Survey of the River Detroit from Lake Erie to Lake St. Clair by Capt. W.F.W Owen & Assistants in 1815* (Apr. 12, 1828), https://recherche-collection-search.bac-lac.gc.ca/eng/Home/Search?q=%20A%20Survey%20of%20the%20River%20Detroit%20from%20Lake%20Erie%20to%20Lake%20St%20Clair%201815 (reference for figure 12.1).

Bruce A. Manny & Thomas A. Edsall, U.S. Fish and Wildlife Service, The Detroit River: An Ecological Profile of Michigan, fig 13 (Distribution of wetlands and large submerged macrophyte beds in the Detroit River (Apr. 1988), *available at* https://www.google.com/books/edition/The_Detroit_River_Michigan/kcCG3Mch-k0C?hl=en&gbpv=1&dq=Manny+et+al.+1988&pg=PR7&printsec=frontcover (reference for figure 12.1).

Michigan Dep't of Environment, Great Lakes, and Energy, *Wetlands Map Viewer*, https://www.mcgi.state.mi.us/wetlands/mcgiMap.html (last visited Nov. 6, 2023) (reference for figure 12.1).

Michigan State University, Michigan Natural Features Inventory, *Michigan c1800 Viewer*, https://mnfi.maps.arcgis.com/apps/webappviewer/index.html?id=bbdca9029f184571bd0369cb4aa90cd2 (last visited Nov. 6, 2023) (reference for figure 12.1).

Ontario GeoHub, *Wetlands*, https://geohub.lio.gov.on.ca/datasets/5216a770ef684d2fae8bcc13ee9c4357/explore?location=42.211281%2C-83.048478%2C13.00 (last updated Nov. 6, 2023) (reference for figure 12.1).

Progressive AE, Management Plan for Lake Lansing and Its Watershed (2002), https://www.meridian.mi.us/home/showpublisheddocument/12538/636614752440900000.

Evelyn Huber Raphael, A History of the Haslett-Lake Lansing Area, Meridian Township, Ingham County, Michigan (1958, revised 1974) (distributed by the Haslett Women's Club).

J.C. Reindl, *Michigan's Golf Course Boom Is Now a Painful Bust*, Detroit Free Press (Apr. 11, 2016), https://www.freep.com/story/money/business/michigan/2016/04/10/michigans-golf-course-boom-now-painful-bust/82755574/.

Telephone Interviews and E-mail Correspondence With Terry Sack (Oct. 15 - Dec. 12, 2022).

Allan Tucker, *The Relation of Phytoplankton Periodicity to the Nature of the Physico-Chemical Environment with Special Reference to Phosphorus. II. Seasonal and Vertical Distribution of the Phytoplankton in Relation to the Environment*, 57 Am. Midland Naturalist 334-70 (1957), https://doi.org/10.2307/2422404.

Wikipedia, *Michigan Meridian*, https://en.wikipedia.org/wiki/Michigan_meridian (last edited May 19, 2023).

Chapter 13
More Swamp Talk

Once through college, Sam gained employment with Michigan State University (MSU) in the campus planning department. His first assignment involved completing a design for an indoor interpretive exhibit entitled "Eutrophication of Glacial Lake Basins." It would be installed in the visitor center at Hidden Lake Gardens, an arboretum spread over more than 600 acres, owned by MSU near Adrian, Michigan. Work started by a previous employee laid out a general concept for the display, but many details remained unfinished. Dr. Parmelee, an in-house scientist, assisted Sam with factual narrations to accompany his illustrations.

Dr. Parmelee's knowledge widely covered the plant world and details about natural ecosystems. In casual conversation, he expressed in-depth warnings about the ongoing destruction of tropical rain forests in Brazil, making points about this area being the lungs of our planet and how its ruin will disrupt the balance between oxygen and carbon dioxide (CO_2). He explained how in this ecosystem, most of the carbon is held in the plant tops, above ground, and very little is stored in the shallow root systems or soil. So, when rain forests are burned, poof, the carbon is released, and the remaining soil is nonproductive, making restoration next to impossible. Carbon storage in rain forests is quite different from the deep sinks of carbon-rich soil in prairies and wetlands of North America.

In the late 1970s, when Dr. Parmelee spoke of this looming disaster, the idea of climate change was not on many people's radar. Although some news of it was published in scientific journals as early as 1957, it would not be until the 1990s that most scientists thought action was necessary to curb the problem. Unfortunately, opposition from fossil fuel companies and ideologists opposed to government involvement effectively obscured facts, turning the issue into a big debate. So, with frequent and more intense rain events now happening along with more wildfires, plans for mitigation and adaptation are still in the talking phase.

The final artwork for the glacial lake basin display illustrates and narrates the process of eutrophication. The story starts with how ice blocks broke away from the last glacier that covered the northeast United States and became buried in sediment. After the blocks melted, resulting in "kettle lakes," a wide variety of plants invaded the shorelines. Over time, these plants were sorted out to become unique "plant communities" based on evolving conditions that suited each surviving plant's individual needs related to moisture, temperature, and soil acidity.

How water flows into a kettle lake affects the soil acidity around the lake and the future makeup of a mature lake's plant community. Soil in and around lakes that are higher in elevation than surrounding land or are lacking an inlet stream generally become acidic, while lakes fed by rivers or streams, with an outlet, generally become neutral to slightly alkaline due to the inward flow of nutrients and ample exchange of oxygen.

As invading shrubs and emergent plants such as arrowheads, rushes, and water lilies surround a lake's perimeter, their dieback and regrowth results in an annual production of dead plant material. In an elevated lake with no inlet and outlet, these remains fall into the lake's nutrient-deficient rainwater. Without the aid of nutrients, these plants decompose slowly. In addition, nutrient-free lakes without water flowing through them typically are anoxic (lacking oxygen). The presence of oxygen is necessary for fungal and microbial activity that promotes decomposition. So, as complete decomposition

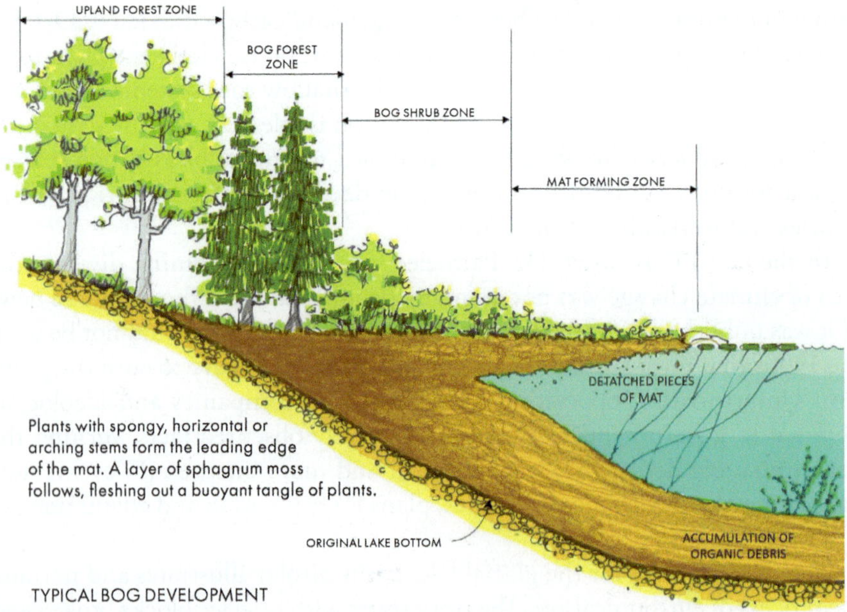

Figure 13.1. Sectional diagram showing bog development.

of dead plant material is prevented, the process results in the formation of "peat," a lightweight, acidic, organic material that floats to the surface and intermingles with the other floating debris. The floating material eventually develops into a tangled mat next to the shore, especially on smaller lakes where wave action is absent. As the mat thickens, it is colonized by new acid-loving plants thriving on the peat-laden growing medium—further perpetuating the buildup of the mat's acidity. The vegetative mat (or bog) is held together by a live root system as it slowly advances outward from the lake edge, capable of eventually closing off the entire lake surface. Slow decay and disturbances on the bottom side of the mat cause waterlogged pieces to dislodge. These sink and accumulate on the lake bottom, so the lake is filled from both the bottom up and the top down.

Developing bogs typically lack nitrogen and other nutrients that most plants need, which often results in an interesting community of carnivorous plants that can adapt to these conditions such as pitcher plants, sundews, and bladderworts. These plants obtain nutrients from insects they catch and digest.

Once bog formation is well underway, acid-loving plants take over the surface with *Sphagnum* moss usually the first to become prolific. Following the growth of moss, the bog becomes invaded by various heaths, especially leatherleaf and other acid-loving shrubs like blueberries, cranberries, and huckleberries. As the bog surface becomes structurally stable, trees begin to grow, with larch among the first pioneers. Black spruce may invade the area as well.

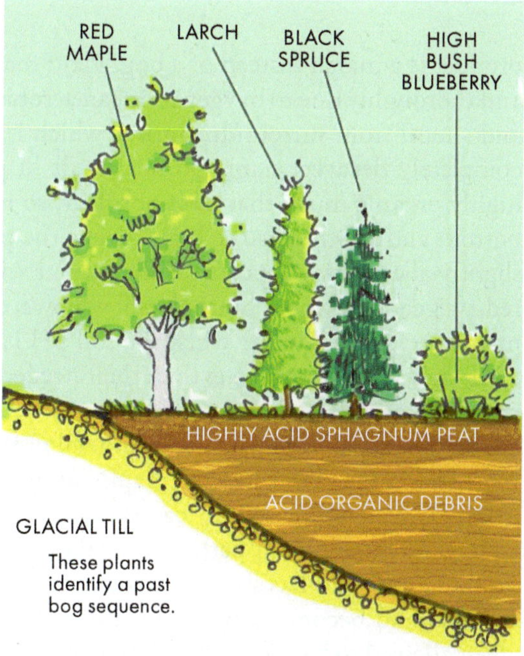

Figure 13.2. Sectional diagram showing a lake terminated by bog development.

Where lakes are lower than the surrounding area and receive water from streams or rivers, the end

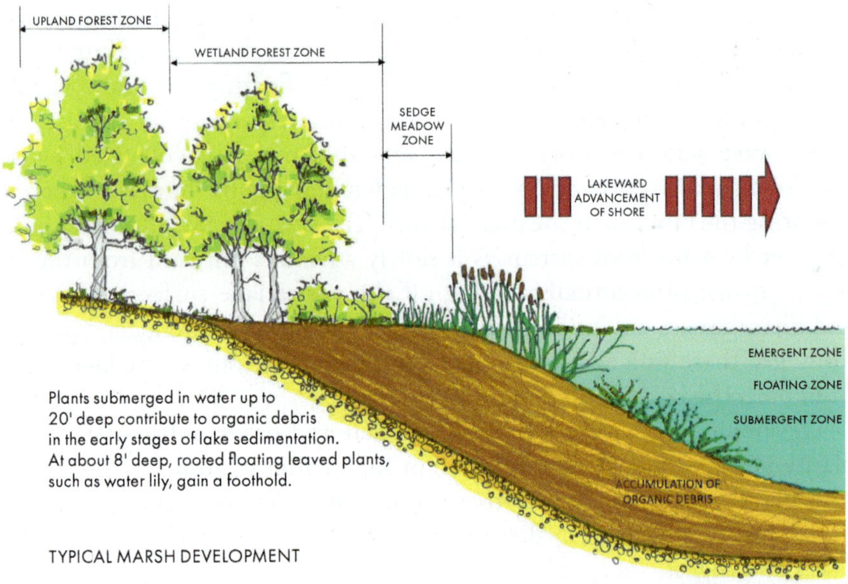

Figure 13.3. Sectional diagram showing marsh development.

product is a marsh instead of a bog. Plant material decomposes more rapidly and thoroughly due to oxygenation (an aerobic condition) from stream inflow and runoff from surrounding areas, which is typically rich in nutrients. The completely decayed plants do not result in peat. Instead, the material is a highly organic muck that does not float, so it immediately drifts to the lake bottom and slowly fills the basin. Since the pH of this material is neutral to slightly alkaline it supports a different but wider variety of plants, including red-twigged dogwood, buttonbush, willows, cottonwoods, and maples. Most plant species are happier when the soil pH is around neutral because at this level, they are best able to extract their needed mineral nutrients. Species that can grow at the raised center of a bog, where it is most acidic, have special adaptation capabilities to obtain mineral nutrients in a low pH environment. Note that some plants like red maple can tolerate a wide range of acidity and moisture availability, so they can show up in various plant community types.

Regardless of which path a lake takes in the eutrophication process, bog or marsh, the end has similar characteristics—the basin fills in with organic material and becomes covered by a distinct plant community. This process, when allowed to happen naturally, can take thousands of years. Yet in the past century, the process is quickening in many glacial lakes, with some already becoming extinct. The reason for this is not a mystery. It is well known that when nutrients in a lake basin—phosphorus in particular—are increased, the eutrophication process accelerates. Phosphorus is important for plant growth. In most lakes, phosphorus is the limiting nutrient, which means that other elements required for plant growth like sunlight, warmth, water, and nitrogen are typically ample. So, as phosphorus is added, the lake can explode with plant growth. Algae, which is required in small doses to support a healthy fishery, can bloom into large, dense masses covering an entire lake's surface, blocking sunlight, and causing an anoxic condition below the bloom. Before long, dead and decayed material from the algae bloom and overly abundant emergent plants fill the lake at a much faster rate than if not stimulated by phosphorus.

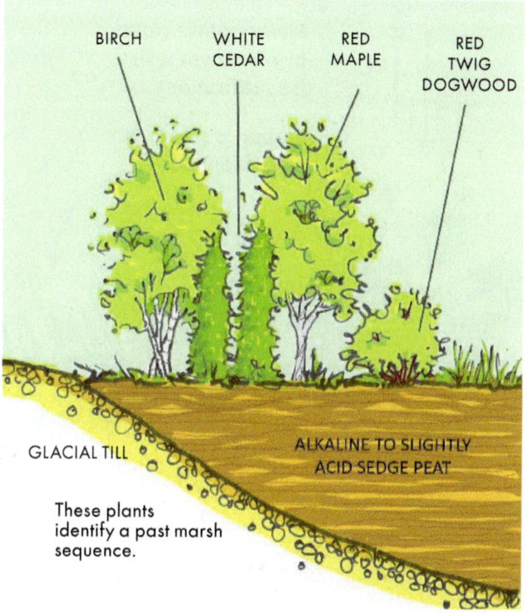

Figure 13.4. Sectional diagram showing a lake terminated by marsh development.

Bogs and marshes represent two kinds of wetlands, both being carbon sinks, meaning they store enormous amounts of carbon by sequestering CO_2 from the atmosphere. With CO_2 being one of the primary greenhouse gases contributing to global warming, wetlands play a key role in keeping carbon secured underground—a fundamental strategy to mitigate the climate change process.

Unfortunately, if wetlands are dredged or drained (dried out) their organic material can oxidize and release carbon back into the atmosphere. Bogs, unlike other wetlands, take thousands of years to develop and hundreds of years to recover. More than 75% of England's bogs are now gone due to extensive peat extraction. In addition to losing climate change mitigation qualities, draining a bog for development or peat extraction also destroys its wildlife habitat value and ability to support biodiversity.

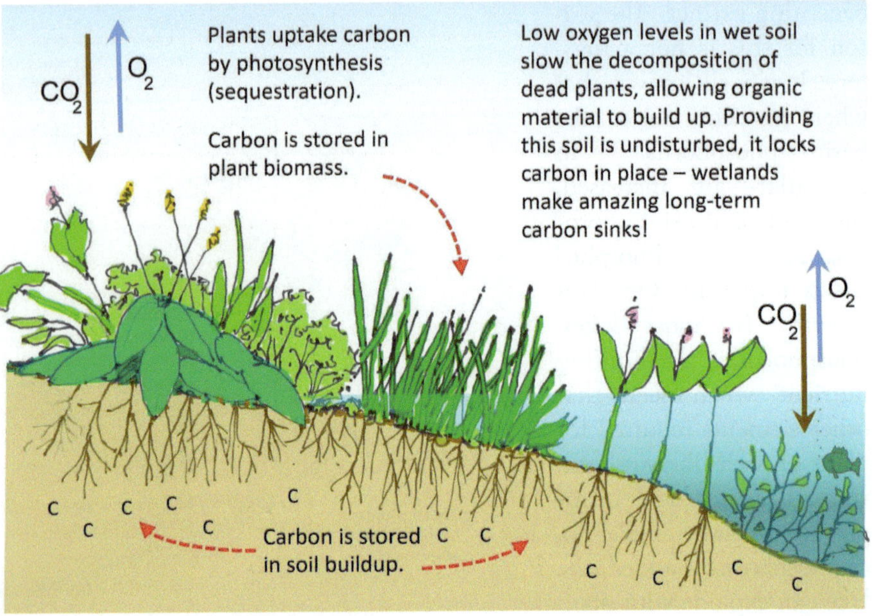

Figure 13.5. Wetlands are highly efficient carbon sinks and can help mitigate climate change.

Wetlands in the continental United States are estimated to store 13.5 billion metric tons of carbon. Freshwater inland wetlands, in part due to their substantial acreage, hold nearly 10 times more carbon than tidal coastal wetlands. Peatlands in forested regions of the East and upper Midwest store the most carbon, accounting for nearly half the wetland carbon in the United States.

Worldwide, peat bogs sequester more than 200 billion tons of carbon, mostly trapped in semi-frozen tundra and boreal forests in Scandinavia and Siberia. As the Siberian tundra and its bogs thaw, millions of tons of carbon and other greenhouse gases, such as methane, a gas that is 25 times more potent than CO_2 in terms of greenhouse effect, will likely be released into the atmosphere. Recent rising temperatures are already cited as a cause of random explosions in Siberian permafrost. Based on warmer ground temperatures, some Russian scientists claim that giant craters discovered in the thawing permafrost are triggered by underground pockets of gas that spontaneously ignite and blow up.

Recent research shows the Arctic is warming faster than previously thought—four times faster than the rest of the world. When people talk about a "tipping point," the irreversible thaw of arctic bogs along with fires in associated boreal forests are seen as contributing events turning these massive carbon sinks into carbon releases and accelerating the rate of climate change further out of control.

Wildfires have become common in the western United States and Canada; however, fire statistics are worsening every year, with 2023's events among the most appalling. Canadian provinces including Alberta, British Columbia, Nova Scotia, Ontario, Quebec, Saskatchewan, and the Northwest Territories all reported fires burning out of control, sending plumes of smoke over nearly all North America. Degraded air quality caused the evacuation of tens of thousands of people, and more than 10 million acres burned by the middle of June. Excessive heat and severe drought in densely forested areas, due to global warming, enhanced conditions and increased chances for fires, which were mostly ignited either by lightning strikes or sparks from passing trains, or by people not putting out campfires, discarding cigarette butts, having automobile accidents, and lighting fireworks.

What's worse than these forest fires is the slow burn of bogs—the combustion of Canadian peatlands. When fire gets into peat and starts smoldering, it's extremely difficult to extinguish and remains burning for long periods of time—even throughout winter, under snow, and then popping up flames the following spring. At least 20 percent of Alberta is covered with peat ecosystems, and the Northwest Territories hosts nearly one-fifth of Canada's peatlands, which scientists say are extremely valuable due to their capacity to store carbon. About 24 billion tonnes of carbon stored in approximately 230,000 square kilometers of land in the Northwest Territories roughly equals the carbon that can be emitted from 200 billion barrels of oil.

Unfortunately, wetlands and especially bogs have received little credit for anything good until recently. For thousands of years, people typically avoided bogs, holding superstitions about them being haunted places. Their spongy and sometimes smoke-releasing soil induced mysterious stories among previous cultures. Finding bog bodies added to the creepiness. These are the remains of people who either died in bogs or were tossed there after being killed—sometimes in multiple ways. The lack of oxygen and acidic soil in bogs along with heavy tannins and cold temperatures act as an excellent preservative, accounting for hundreds of bog bodies discovered throughout northern Europe. They range from children to the elderly, with some having leather ropes around their necks or large portions of their bodies missing. All this contributed to conspiracy theories indicating bogs are bad places.

Poor soil quality, lack of drainage, and biting insects rendered bogs and marshes useless into the 1960s. This perception held true for the wetland surrounding Mud Lake. It was so swampy it seemed to be part bog and part marsh! Some of the edge areas would jiggle like Jell-O with every step and have weak spots, where if one slipped through, they would quickly be standing on the lake bottom—hopefully with their head still above the vegetation. Observations of pitcher plants were also reported, suggesting bog development. Yet, with a defined inlet and outlet, bringing oxygenated water and minerals into the lake, marsh development is more likely the lake's dominant eutrophication route.

The massive wetland surrounding Mud Lake withstood the pressure of urban development and continues to provide the great service of sequestering and storing carbon. However, the immense loss of wetlands worldwide is catastrophic. Scientists are telling us that significant reductions of carbon emissions along with aggressive protection and restoration of plant-dominated ecosystems are required to restore a balance within the carbon budget. Large "green infrastructure" swaths of all kinds including forests, prairies, and wetlands are needed to recreate lost carbon sinks.

For Steve, Sam, Beth, and their friends, the marsh around Mud Lake could be seen from the O'Bryant farm fence—marshy, boggy, and muddy—and tales circulated about cows getting stuck, needing to be rescued, or even dying in the muck. Probably not true, but the stories and language used about the landscape—swamp, muck, black dirt, and images of cows consumed by mud—reflected common negative attitudes about the value of wetland environments at that time—something undesirable and best to be filled in. "Wetland" was not part of the local vocabulary. "Swamp" was the common term. Ironically, while people accepted negative perceptions about wetlands without thought, the reality of this landscape, the water, the life, the sensuous seasonal explosion of growth and gradual senescence of the dense plant life, attracted children like a magnet.

In October 1965, a *Meridian News* headline announced, "Board Adopts Flood Plain Ordinance." The township board had adopted the first floodplain ordinance in the state of Michigan. Rod Hagenbuch, a newbie to the board with no formal training in environmental or planning matters, drafted the ordinance with guidance from an expert who worked in the state government. Not all the benefits of wetlands were appreciated at this time, but people were beginning to wake up to the idea about how taking them away eliminates water storage areas during heavy rain events, resulting in flooding of developed land.

The ordinance identified all land in the township that went under water during a 100-year flood, and these properties became subject to new restrictions. Instead of totally banning floodplain development, which was not a popular idea, Rod offered a solution permitting development in the floodplain providing that any filling would be compensated by an equal or greater amount of excavated soil to maintain the original water storage capacity.

Years later, Rod learned that the expert in the state government who counseled him with Meridian Township's ordinance had been trying, without success, to get the state to address protection of floodplains. With the Meridian ordinance in the books, he finally convinced government officials to pass statewide floodplain laws using some of the same concepts and language contained in the Meridian floodplain ordinance.

Interestingly, at the same time Mud Lake was lapping at the back of Rod's home, he was writing Meridian's floodplain ordinance, but still, by his own admission, he and his colleagues remained unaware of even the word "wetland" and all the environmental services wetlands provide. Later, they realized the ordinance helped protect against flooding but did not protect wetland ecosystems. It wasn't until 1979 that the Michigan Legislature effectively protected wetlands by passing the Geomare-Anderson Wetlands Protection Act. This was amended in 1994 to become Part 303, Wetlands Protection, of the Natural Resources and Environmental Protection Act.

References

Bog, Britannica, https://www.britannica.com/science/bog-wetland (last updated Mar. 11, 2023).

Victoria Gill & Ella Hambly, *Climate Change: Dimming Earth, Mustard Shortages, and Other Odd Side-effects*, BBC (Nov. 12, 2022), https://www.bbc.com/news/science-environment-63585043.

Telephone Interviews and E-mail Correspondence With Beth Hagenbuch, Landscape Architect (Feb. 11 - Apr. 5, 2022).

Rodney Hagenbuch, Rodney Hagenbuch Memoir (1965) (unpublished manuscript).

Joshua Levine, *Europe's Famed Bog Bodies Are Starting to Reveal Their Secrets*, Smithsonian Mag. (May 2017), https://www.smithsonianmag.com/science-nature/europe-bog-bodies-reveal-secrets-180962770/.

Isabella Kaminski, *Did climate change cause Canada's wildfires? Isabella Kaminski digs into the science on the role climate change and other factors play in wildfires*, BBC, (June 12, 2023), https://www.bbc.com/future/article/20230612-did-climate-change-cause-canadas-wildfires.

Liny Lamberink, *N.W.T. peatlands store 24 billion tonnes of carbon and are worth protecting, experts say,* CBC News, (Dec 6, 2021), https://www.cbc.ca/news/canada/north/peatlands-nwt-carbon-protection-1.6273262

Minnesota Board of Water and Soil Resources, *Carbon Sequestration in Wetlands*, https://bwsr.state.mn.us/carbon-sequestration-wetlands (last visited May 31, 2023).

National Geographic, *Bog*, https://education.nationalgeographic.org/resource/bog (last visited May 31, 2023).

National Park Service, *Wetlands, Marshes, and Swamps*, https://www.nps.gov/piro/learn/nature/wetlands.htm (last updated Sept. 22, 2021).

Ridah Syed, *How many fires are burning, how did they start and other answers to questions about wildfires in Canada,* Milwaukee J. Sentinal (June 28, 2023), https://www.jsonline.com/story/news/2023/06/28/what-to-know-about-the-ongoing-canadian-wildfires/70364230007/.

Julia Wong, *Wildfires in peat an added challenge for Alberta firefighters,* CBC News, (May 22, 2023), https://www.cbc.ca/news/canada/edmonton/wildfires-peat-challenge-alberta-firefighters-1.6850347

Chapter 14
Wetlands, Glaciers, and Climate Change

The completed "Eutrophication of Glacial Lake Basins" interpretive exhibit shows eutrophication as a linear process, yet because glaciers keep coming and going and as new lakes are formed with every passing ice mass, lake creation is actually a cyclical event synchronized with glacial occurrences. The ice age we are now experiencing, which has dragged on for three million years, had multiple relatively warm periods with minimal glacial coverage called "interglacial" periods. These alternated with "glacial" periods when the ice sheet dipped deep into areas now known as Ohio and Illinois. We are enjoying an interglacial period today with the last cold spell ending about 11,000 years ago. That was a tough time to be alive, although woolly mammoth hunting was apparently quite good.

Cave paintings were also popular in those days, with some of the most famous ones done in southern France between 17,000 and 20,000 years ago—definitely a chilly time period. The Chauvet Cave in this region is probably the greatest Paleolithic painted cave ever discovered. Interestingly, almost all artwork in these caves illustrates wildlife, with many extinct mammals included, underscoring the human affinity for the natural world, even when we were more integrally a part of it.

In relation to "geological time," movements between glacial and interglacial periods, within a single ice age, are quick blips. Scientists tell us this movement back and forth happened at least four times in the past 450,000 years prior to the interglacial period that is dishing out great weather today. Since human beings have been living on earth for about 300,000 years, they have experienced several of these changes between glacial and interglacial periods within our three-million-year-old ice age.

Average temperatures near the earth's poles change at least 10 degrees between glacial and interglacial periods. In addition to these significant temperature swings, minor temperature fluctuations occur within both glacial and interglacial periods. The last heat wave during our current interglacial period is speculated to have occurred during the Middle Ages in which rela-

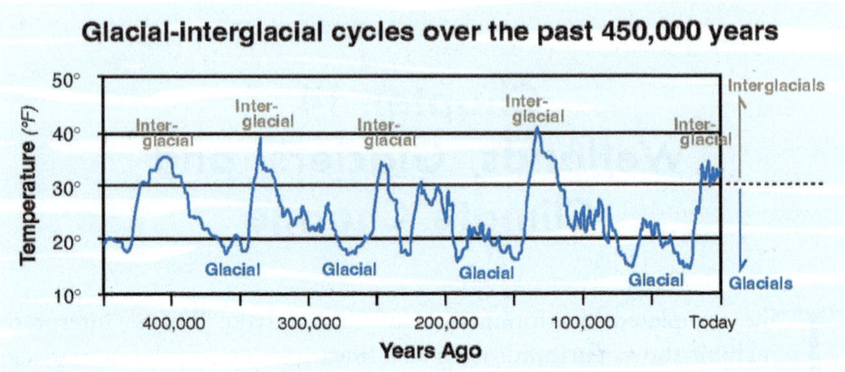

Figure 14.1. Interglacial cycles (10,000 to 30,000 years long) alternate with much longer and much colder glacial cycles (70,000 to 90,000 years long). Cooling periods leading up to glacial periods appear to be gradual, while temperature swings into warmer, interglacial periods are more abrupt. Shown temperatures are latitude-specific (e.g., Antarctica, Alaska, Greenland) temperature changes inferred from Antarctic ice cores (not global averages).
Credit: Sandy Eldredge and Bob Biek, Utah Geological Survey, Glad You Asked: Ice Ages – What Are They and What Causes Them?.

tively warm conditions prevailed in various parts of the world. During this time, agricultural practices and production flourished along with many other benefits for people in the Northern Hemisphere from Greenland eastward through Europe and parts of Asia. However, in other parts of the world like Central America, people's lives were made worse by intense droughts. History proved we can survive this kind of change, although its cause had nothing to do with humans releasing too much greenhouse gas into the atmosphere. Instead, it likely resulted from a change in El Niño—a recurring climate pattern of winds and sea-surface temperatures over the Tropical Eastern Pacific. And since temperatures experienced since 2000 in the Northern Hemisphere are already hotter than any time during the medieval warm period, it looks like our global warming is something different than what happened a millennium ago.

So, with all these minor climate changes occurring over the past few million years, prior to the change we are now experiencing, it is apparent that humans had nothing to do with any of them. In fact, they seem to be going in cycles entirely on their own, assuming a few cave fires did not release enough carbon to cause any previous warm-ups.

Looking back over a longer time line, at least five major ice ages occurred in the past 2.4 billion years separated by long ultra-hot spells. The most recent hot period, known as the Jurassic Period, lasted well over 100 million years and ended long before humans showed up. Minor temperature changes that occur within an ice age are one thing, which may be tolerable, but a drastic temperature rise out of our comfy ice age, with average global temperatures kicking up another 20 degrees Fahrenheit, could be catastrophic for all life on earth as we know it—brontosaurus stew anyone? Just watch out for the pterosaurs.

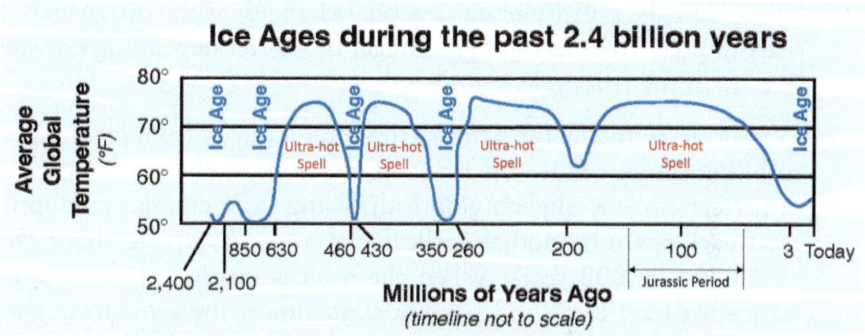

Figure 14.2. Chart showing when five major ice ages occurred in the past 2.4 billion years of Earth's history. Modified from several sources including Dynamical Paleoclimatology: Generalized Theory of Global Climate Change, 2002, by Barry Saltzman.

Credit: Modified from Sandy Eldredge and Bob Biek, Utah Geological Survey, Glad You Asked: Ice Ages – What Are They and What Causes Them?

So, what causes these more drastic temperature swings? Many factors come into play, including changes in oceanic and atmospheric circulation patterns, varying concentrations of atmospheric carbon dioxide, and volcanic eruptions. A significant cause of major ice ages is the changing positions of earth's ever-moving continents, which affect oceanic and atmospheric circulation patterns. When continent arrangement impedes warm water flow from the equator to the poles, ice sheets may develop and set an ice age in motion. Today's ice age likely began when the land bridge between North and South America (Isthmus of Panama) formed, which ended warm water flow between the Atlantic and Pacific Oceans, significantly rerouting ocean currents.

Less drastic temperature swings between glacial and interglacial periods, within ice ages, occur in fairly regular cycles. Most scientists believe that a Serbian astrophysicist, Milutin Milanković, came up with a reasonable theory to explain these changes, based on cyclical variations in three aspects of earth's orbit around the sun that affect our seasons and cause minor changes in solar radiation intensity reaching earth. According to Milanković, these cycles include:

1. Changes in the tilt of the earth's axis: Right now, the axis of our spin is tilted at about 23.5 degrees from vertical, but this can vary by a degree or so either way. This total variation of about 2.4 degrees happens on a 41,000-year cycle. Seemingly insignificant, this slight change in our tilt affects the severity of our seasonal changes, as the distance of the earth's poles from the sun gets longer or shorter depending on where we are in the "tilt cycle."
2. Variations in the shape of the earth's orbit: Gravity from other planets orbiting the sun cause the shape of our orbit to change from almost a perfect circle to slightly elliptical. Going from circular to elliptical and back again is another cyclical movement occurring about every 100,000-400,000 years. When the orbit is nearly circular, the distance between earth and the sun stays almost the same throughout the year, which keeps the amount of solar energy reaching earth at a constant level. But when the orbit is more elliptical, the distance between the earth and sun along with the amount of energy reaching earth changes between seasons, causing slightly warmer or cooler temperatures. Today, earth's orbit is much closer to being circular than elliptical, which correlates with us enjoying an interglacial period for the past 11,000 years. And if history repeats itself, or if these alternating warm and cold periods within an ice age are truly cyclical, we should be on an ultra-slow downward dip to another glacial period—back to woolly mammoth and saber-toothed tiger jerky.
3. Changes in the earth's wobble: Earth's axis of rotation wanders in a circular movement like a spinning top that is slowing down, giving it a slow wobble. The rotational axis wobbles back and forth between pointing at two stars—Polaris and Vega. This wobble, which completes a full cycle about every 26,000 years, acts similar to the earth's change in tilt by changing the distance of the earth's poles from the sun as it goes along its orbit, again affecting (actually compounding) the severity of our seasonal changes, which impacts periods of glaciation.

If Milanković's theories are fact, we probably can't do much to stop these "natural" climate changes. However, the Milankovitch cycles are extremely slow moving and take from tens of thousands to hundreds of thousands of years to make any significant temperature change. In contrast, earth's current warming is happening quickly, taking place over the past 150 years. Milankovitch cycles have changed the amount of solar energy absorbed by earth very little during this time, and, in fact, National Aeronautics and Space Administration (NASA) satellite observations show that recent solar radiation due to these cycles has actually decreased somewhat. Since our global temperatures are going in the wrong direction, and the only rational answer for temperatures going up is a noticeable increase in greenhouse gas emissions, which we have unnaturally caused, there might be something we can do to stop or slow the process. Conversely, if there is a natural reason that we are jumping out of our ice age into another ultra-hot and steamy period, why would we want to accelerate the process?

Eutrophication of glacial lake basins and the climate change we are now witnessing appear to have a common thread—both are accelerated by human activity. And the acceleration can go wildly out of control once a tipping point is reached. Like slowly applying pressure on a light switch, when the point of no return is reached, the switch turns off, and it's lights out!

Scientists are telling us we are now heading for the climate change tipping point, as the rise in greenhouse gas emissions is consistent with some previous major ice age departures. Could we be lucky enough to find our melting ice caps might cool our oceans enough to reverse global temperatures into a downward trend, perpetuating our ice age—only to cause centuries of catastrophic flood damage along our coastlines but not total world destruction? Or maybe it will just be several decades of more frequent and intense rain events, flooding, and wildfires causing famine and death without discriminating. Either way, much time is being wasted in the debate about the seriousness of our predicament.

Regardless of what terrible thing happens next, it appears that we are beyond mitigating the problem and need to develop "adaptation" strategies. Unfortunately, our adaptation skills are slow at best. Let's face it, more than 200 years have passed since our country's Declaration of Independence clearly stated, "All men are created equal," yet the idea is still met with resistance by many. So far, reducing carbon emissions and reestablishing carbon sinks are the only strategies known to slow the global warming process down while we rebuild infrastructure in sustainable locations. And like the equal rights issue, we are still caught up in conversations about the reality of our problem.

References

Alan Buis, *Milankovitch (Orbital) Cycles and Their Role in Earth's Climate*, NASA Glob. Climate Change (Feb. 27, 2020), https://climate.nasa.gov/news/2948/milankovitch-orbital-cycles-and-their-role-in-earths-climate/.

Alan Buis, *Why Milankovitch (Orbital) Cycles Can't Explain Earth's Current Warming*, NASA Glob. Climate Change (Feb. 27, 2020), https://climate.nasa.gov/ask-nasa-climate/2949/why-milankovitch-orbital-cycles-cant-explain-earths-current-warming/.

Sandy Eldredge & Bob Biek, *Glad You Asked: Ice Ages—What Are They and What Causes Them?*, Surv. Notes (Utah Geological Survey, Salt Lake City, Utah), Sept. 2019, https://geology.utah.gov/map-pub/survey-notes/glad-you-asked/ice-ages-what-are-they-and-what-causes-them/.

Chapter 15
One More Ride Down Roller Coaster Hill

The greater Mud Lake landscape offered multiple features to challenge and enhance mental and physical capabilities of the neighborhood kids. Cricket (Chris) Earley's athletic ability did not just start happening during his junior year in high school. Challenges presented by the natural attractions surrounding Mud Lake provided high-quality agility and strength training—and testing, with failure often resulting in distress. A favorite place to measure progress, known as the Pines, laid along the railroad tracks, near Wilkshire Elementary School, at the edge of a large open field. Cricket knew all the nooks and crannies in this stand of trees. His family's first home in the Mud Lake area, before moving to Orlando Drive, was on Haslett Road across the street from the open field.

This conifer grove almost exclusively contained Norway spruce, but since none of the neighborhood youngsters knew the difference between pines and spruces, and "pine" was the go-to term for any evergreen tree, "the Pines" undisputedly became the name for this place. The trees were densely planted and nearly fully grown, making a walk through them a challenge on its own. A dark, cooling shade and rich scent of spruce resin created an ambiance like no other in the Mud Lake area. Small openings with some linked together by narrow passageways created a maze-like environment where everything looked the same, so it was easy to lose your orientation. It was a great place to play anything that involved hiding, such as war games or capture the flag. Once out of the trees, along the grove's north edge, before reaching the railroad tracks, the ground dropped off into swampland with plenty of standing water—no telling how deep in some places. Remnants of the interurban track that ran from Lansing to Perry and up to Owosso could be found in this swamp, making an outstanding challenge course, especially where it passed through deep water. Jumping from one deteriorating track support beam to another separated daring kids from chickens.

"Capture the flag" became a popular game in the dark green labyrinth with a forgiving floor of spruce needles. As many as 15 to 20 players would attend each event. Cricket held a slight advantage over most—being a little shorter than average, he quickly navigated under low branches and through tight spaces. However, during one full tilt run, trying not to be captured, he stumbled and fell headfirst into a tree, knocking himself silly and scraping his face up pretty good.

During another arduous capture the flag episode, Bobby Fotchman was heard screaming "Help!" at the top of his lungs. After a brief search, Cricket found him perched in a treetop where he claimed to have climbed to escape the clutches of a hobo. Bobby had a flair for drama and pranks, so Cricket and the others had their doubts, but they all started doing over-the-shoulder checks to see what might be lurking behind them as the day continued.

Other attractions at the Pines included a couple of dump sites providing interesting places to pick around in. Findings in these junk piles like empty whiskey bottles substantiated kid's lore about "hobos" that camped in the trees. A rather deep swale running north and south through the Pines contained one of the junk piles. With all the good stuff already snatched up, nothing much of any value remained. It was mostly a pile of old, rusty tin cans and broken glass bottles, although it still attracted search parties when there was nothing better to do. If one chose not to waste time looking for something special, a log spanned over the swale, making a quick way to get over it. Here is where Cricket loses another of his many battles against gravity. When in hot pursuit of an opposing team's flag, making use of this log bridge seems like a no-brainer. Unfortunately, in Cricket's haste, the log rotates when he is about halfway across, sending him into the cans and broken bottles below. Sixteen stitches and one tetanus shot later, his left arm was immobilized in bandages for the next month.

Closer to home after a recent snowfall, Cricket, Mark, and Dennis spent a Saturday afternoon climbing on the roof of a two-story house that was under construction across the street from the Shinns' place. Again, Cricket loses his footing and starts sliding off the roof, grasping at anything to avoid going over the edge. Screaming the whole way, he eventually lands on a snow-covered pile of construction debris about 15 feet down. Mark could not resist laughing during the entire event. Fortunately, there was no damage to the roof or Cricket.

When roaming around the east side of Mud Lake with his older brother, Rob, gravity pulls another punch. Misjudging the distance between sedge mounds before hopping from one to the next results in a deep slip into the muck. With Cricket submerged above his waist, Rob had to pull him out. After considerable effort, everything came up except for one shoe that was sucked from his foot and never recovered. Rob insists that Cricket would have died that day if he hadn't been there.

Likewise, Mark absorbed an assortment of survival tactics from this awesome outdoor environment. Although gifted with more intelligence than most people, Mud Lake-area adventures offered up regular events conditioning him to make safe decisions. Shinnying up the first 20 feet of the water tower to latch onto the ladder confirmed his athleticism, even without going any further. And if anyone disagreed, he could prove it in a footrace.

One summer day most of the Orlando Street Gang had congregated in Hank Parker's backyard, enjoying the shade of a large oak tree and some freshly plucked carrots from Mrs. Parker's garden, wiped almost clean by shirt sleeves. Before they could get to the green beans, the notion of climbing a nearby willow tree in the neighbor's yard originated from Jim Bissell. Jim was a Hallendale Road resident who occasionally jumped around with Steve, Brent, and other kids in the multi-stem boxelder tree between Buckingham Road and Coral Way. Jim shared a family trait with the boxelder tree jump champion, Steve—they both had older brothers who could easily tear your arm off and beat you with it. So, daring tree jumps and other survival tests came naturally to Jim. Yet he could show a gentle side as well. He and Brent spent hours playing baseball, using a tennis ball instead of a hard ball, with Becky and her next-door friend, Diane. Sam Sr. had planted four trees as whips in his backyard that served as the infield diamond. A tree-of-heaven was first base, a mulberry tree was second, a willow tree was third, and any flat object or extra clothing that was handy, placed near an apple tree, served as home plate. If you hit into Diane's mom's garden it was an automatic out, but past the garden and over the fence was a home run. And the girls got four swings—that was it for special rules, otherwise it was serious tennis baseball.

So, with minimal discussion about Jim's proposal to climb the willow, the boys sprint to the tree and start climbing like monkeys as though it was a race to the top. Mark probably had the ability to win but hangs back a bit, based on nearly falling out of this tree in the past. Jim takes the lead and, before long, reaches where the trunk moved dramatically with every puff of wind. Then, without warning, Jim suddenly flies past Mark in a downward direction, changing only slightly with each branch he bounces against before slamming into the lawn. Luckily, the fall only breaks his arm, but with the resulting cast, putting Jim on the injured list, there would be no more tennis baseball with Becky, Brent, and Diane for the rest of the season. Snake catching in the Woods was still doable, however, and with Jim's mother no longer getting milk deliveries, the milk box on his back porch, half-filled with grass clippings, made a suitable holding pen. Jim's flight downward along with all the branches he dislodged on his way fortunately missed the other climbers. So, after packing him up for his trip to Doc Siddall's office, the crew returned to the veggie garden to snack on green beans. With all the interruptions that day, there would be no time to taunt the bull near Mud Lake.

In addition to Mark's driveway basketball court, Mark's father thoughtfully planted two tart cherry trees on opposite sides of their rear yard that perfectly identified goal lines for football contests. Visiting teams included Steve and Brent's gang from the Buckingham/Coral Way block and a group from the Wilkshire subdivision. This team was brutal. Their star player, although no older than anyone else, was full grown at age 11. Bumps, bruises, and bloody noses happened regularly, as these were always no-equipment events. Like all "games" for kids growing up in the 1950s and early '60s, helmets and pads for football, hockey, skateboarding, roller-skating, baseball—you name it—were not even imagined for the younger age group.

Mark's affinity for turtle catching ranked high on his free-time agenda. So, he was frequently found patrolling the banks of First Creek in the company of his pals or on his own. Since most turtles seemed to linger on the other side of the wire fence running along the road's east side, someone remodeled the fence mesh with an opening large enough for crawling through. With elderberries and other wetland shrubs providing camouflage, passage through the opening could happen unnoticed by a passing motorist, which was rare. Nevertheless, almost every fencepost displayed a "no trespassing" sign, and no one wanted to debate why those signs did not apply to kids under 12.

On the wild side of the fence is where Mark spotted the most unusual turtle yet seen in the creek—of course, sunbathing on the opposite bank. The wire fence that passed through the creek made a convenient way to cross without wading, but due to its flimsy structure and rusty barbed wire, it took some skill to avoid falling or getting scraped by the wire. Mark proved his daring to the gang in the past by clambering across the creek while clinging to the fence, so another trip on the wire seemed like the best way to approach the turtle. At about midway, the mesh begins pulling away from the posts, turning it from vertical to a near-horizontal position, with him on the underside. Grabbing for anything stable, the barbed wire gets in the way, and suddenly Mark is swimming. Keeping minimal composure, he still manages to grab the turtle.

Mark recognized this catch to be a prize and took it home for a pet. He was excited to learn its identity from his mother as a box turtle—rare in this area. However, he was taken aback by her displeasure about him being scratched up and covered with mud from head to toe. Worse yet, she did not want him to keep the turtle. So, after fruitless discussion, the "pet" was returned to the creek later that day under supervision of his smiling dad.

All these experiences, although difficult at the time, created lasting impressions and common lifetime memories shared by the boys and their buddies. Each one prepared them for a next situation that would require a mental or physical test. Electronic games of today are missing the bold reality of the greater Mud Lake area—a real place, with real plants, wildlife, people, and pain. The educational and physical training that comes with this kind of environment, although subtle, is second to none.

With all these real-life experiences, the 1960s and '70s kids are best informed to handle today's survival challenges. Likewise, they are the people that should know the truth about climate change. They are the ones that witnessed all the subtle incremental changes over the last three quarters of a century and can remember when it was normal to play at least one late-season high school football game in the snow every year; when having open water on the pond by the end of December was unheard of; and when air conditioning was a rarity for homes and non-existent in automobiles—and no one melted.

What's more, they benefited from biodiversity longer than most people living today. They were healed by medicines derived from obscure plant species, nurtured by our agricultural industry that relies on thousands of pollinating species, and received the most exposure to natural outdoor spaces rich with diverse life now known to improve working memory, attention control, and cognitive flexibility along with enhancing happiness, reducing stress, and promoting overall health and wellbeing. They can remember when uncountable frog fatalities littered roadways on spring mornings following a late-night rainfall, when moths of all sizes and colors were common, when there was no shortage of bees, and when invasive species were more likely regarded as fictional aliens from outer space rather than real critters or plants from a neighboring continent, disrupting our native ecosystems. Now representing the oldest members of most family circles, these people are the most experienced in mending connections when broken. Their words are important to our younger generations.

References

Telephone Interviews and E-mail Correspondence With Chris Earley, Retired Social Worker for the State of Michigan (Mar. 10 - Apr. 14, 2022).

Telephone Interviews and E-mail Correspondence With Becky Goodman, Downtown Director, City of Petoskey (Feb. 22 - Apr. 28, 2022).

Telephone Interviews and E-mail Correspondence With Mark Nimphie, Retired Mechanical/ Electrical Engineer (Mar. 5 - Apr. 14, 2022).

Chapter 16
Going Full Circle

Migrating in Circles

Elephants have wandered Africa for centuries, establishing their migration routes around sources of food, water, and danger. Using their incredible memories to recall these routes, matriarchs of the herd annually guide their families to familiar freshwater and feeding grounds. Travel is largely by night to avoid poaching and other human dangers. Communication methods used to lead the way and give warnings include body gestures, low-frequency vibrations, and chemical secretions.

While wars and poaching have devastated elephant populations, human development is blocking their migratory routes. New farmlands, fences, and reserves have created barriers leading to overpopulation in areas where food supplies are short and with no pathway out.

Food and water become even more scarce when elephant herds are congested, and the landscape becomes damaged due to concentrating their massive weight and destructive lifestyle. Before Europeans began colonizing Africa, there may have been 26 million elephants, and today there are fewer than half a million. The existing landscape certainly cannot support historical numbers, but at the rate they're dwindling, this animal is headed for extinction.

Fortunately, in recent years, African countries such as Kenya, Zambia, Tanzania, Namibia, Botswana, and Zimbabwe, in conjunction with organizations such as Elephants Without Borders and Save the Elephants, have worked to restore some of the elephant migration routes. After working to clear human obstructions and impede poachers, many regions are finding that elephants gradually reclaim their ancient pathways. It appears elephants never forget!

Elephants are not the only animals wandering in circles. Many fish species do it. Birds do it. Caribou do it. Whales do it. Sharks do it. Wildebeests do it. Monarch butterflies do it. And the list goes on—even people do it. Many Native American and early European cultures spent their lives doing it. Today, human migration is less prevalent, as advanced agricultural practices and Amazon deliveries have eliminated much of our need to travel. And for many, COVID squelched our daily trips to work and back. Yet vacation time remains a high priority and often involves repetitive trips to familiar places for nurturing our inner spirits.

The migration of the monarch butterfly might be one of the most inspirational of all migratory movements. According to the World Wildlife Fund, these tiny creatures fly nearly 3,000 miles from southern Canada, where they breed, all the way to the mountain forests of central Mexico, where they hibernate—one of the world's longest migrations. So, it's no wonder they are recognized as symbols of resilience in urban environments and are a welcome "heralding of summer" in rural areas. In Mexico on November 1st and 2nd—the "Day of the Dead"—their arrival has an even deeper meaning. Tradition maintains that monarchs are the returning souls of loved ones. Being so directly connected to the earth's movement around the sun, it is understandable how monarch butterflies represent spiritual evolution and cosmic connection.

Sadly, during the past two decades, monarch butterfly numbers have dramatically declined due to deforestation in Mexico, disruptions to their migration routes, and the loss of nectar-producing native plants along these corridors. Certain species of milkweed, which offer one of their favorite nectars, are typically found in wetlands along with many of their other host plants. And now, after more than a decade of publicizing the monarch's decline, resulting in thousands of people planting milkweed, monarch populations appear to be rising. Although reasons for the recent monarch population increase are not conclusive, they are apparently enjoying the new wildflower gardening trend that includes milkweed.

Declining elephant and monarch butterfly populations represent two examples of how humans negatively interfered with natural cycles. Yet we have seen how deliberate changes in our actions can slow down or possibly stop the extinction process. People are clearly uniquely vested with the ability to influence changes in natural cycles—both harmfully and helpfully.

How People Can Make Change

Negative influences on natural cycles are not typically intentional. Instead, they oftentimes happen as a byproduct of some unrelated action that seems necessary for people to survive or prosper. Filling and hardening the shoreline of the Detroit River seemed like a great thing for our economy during the Industrial Revolution, just like killing all the beaver put money in everyone's pockets in generations prior. And now, burning and lumbering off rain forests are helping to keep mouths fed. However, everyone knows these are all short-term benefit makers having long-term negative consequences.

Positive influences on natural cycles are more challenging because they seem to require actions involving some sort of sacrifice. But this is not always the case. For example, look how the Michigan floodplain ordinance developed. The idea of requiring filled areas in a floodplain to be matched by an equal volume of earth excavation was born out of thinking Meridian Township needed a lot of development to foster a strong economy. Even though imposed restrictions in this ordinance were quite shortsighted, instating only a strategy to allow development in flood zones in a way that would not cause flooding, other more comprehensive wetland protections eventually evolved out of this legislation.

Interestingly, the township's ordinance authors resided near the marsh area around Mud Lake or other wetland in Meridian Township, which has more than its fair share of wet spots. Although having some of the most educated, experienced, and articulate planning commission members in the state regarding wetland issues at that time, their true knowledge regarding wetland science was far from complete. Let's face it, Rod Hagenbuch's experience came from his everyday subconscious interaction with marsh life not willing to stay on the other side of his back property line. Similar interactions resulting in subliminal wetland enchantment were experienced by other commission members living near a Meridian Township swamp as well.

Figure 16.1. Ozz Warbach used cartoons to teach people about nature and wildlife.
Image Credit: Michigan Department of Natural Resources

This phenomenon affected more than a few people living near Mud Lake. Oscar "Ozz" Warbach lived on

Orlando Drive at the corner of Biscayne Way. As a transplant from New Jersey, he became a prominent conservation illustrator for the Michigan Department of Natural Resources (DNR). His appealing style attracted national attention, and the DNR's "Outstanding Partnership Awards" program was initiated in his honor. As suggested by this program's name, Ozz demonstrated outstanding partnership skills with the public by making people aware of environmental and wildlife issues long before this kind of communication was popular.

As everyone knows, good apples don't just roll into the swamp. Ozz's son, John, after graduating from Haslett High School and Michigan State University (MSU), earned his master's degree in landscape architecture from the University of California at Berkeley before returning to MSU to obtain his doctorate in urban forestry. Besides coordinating the Michigan Higher Education Land Policy Consortium, teaching landscape architecture at the State University of New York and MSU, and consulting to governmental units at all levels on a wide range of environmental and land use planning projects, he served on the Lake Lansing Advisory Committee in developing the *Management Plan for Lake Lansing and Its Watershed.*

Milton Baron lived a block to the east of Ozz and John on Buckingham Road. Honored as a "Fellow" in the American Society of Landscape Architects, Milt served MSU as assistant campus landscape architect and as an assistant professor of landscape architecture in the 1960s, later to become the director of Campus Park and Planning before retiring in 1981. He was intricately involved in land planning projects during the campus' extensive southward expansion, and he is recognized as the driving force in developing the campus grounds as an arboretum for learning about plants collected from worldwide locations. These exotic specimens are artistically placed alongside majestic native trees like white pine, sugar maples, red maples, and numerous oak species. Using "education" as the primary motive for funding requests, he successfully implemented impressively diverse tree planting projects as new road and building construction replaced campus-owned farmland. Before "green infrastructure" was heard of or thought to be needed as a measure to mitigate climate change, he was making it happen without knowing it.

Several lots west of the Warbach residence, the Taylor home, on Biscayne Way, overlooked Mud Lake. Jane and her husband tended a beehive near their back lot line, which made great holiday gifts of honey for their neighbors (and paperboy, Brent). Understanding the benefits children can attain by interacting with plants, she designed the award-winning 4-H Children's Garden on MSU's campus in collaboration with Deb Kinney, a landscape architect living on the edge of another Haslett natural area. With numerous national awards, Jane is credited with developing the "children's garden concept," which creatively uses plants in kids' outdoor play spaces. The concept encourages plant engagement similar to what can happen in a natural environment. These places are like botanical gardens, but designed for kids, so that when entering, no one needs to follow the pathways or look without touching. There are no signs with instructions on how to play—only hidden surprises to inspire imagination. Her gardens and others following suit do not directly influence climate change. However, the wizardry associated with these gardens, stemming from unrestricted and creative plant interactions, positively impacts countless kids' minds, opening corridors for further understanding of the natural world later in life.

Hmm. It sounds like these people may have been sniffing a lot of marsh gas. Regardless, it appears that subconscious decisions favoring positive influences on natural cycles have come from the minds of people engaging with Mud Lake and its surroundings.

A Vision for Mud Lake

Today Mud Lake, now called Wildlife Lake, is owned by Haslett Public Schools. When acquired in the early 1970s, visionary educators recognized the value of this 100-acre natural area as a teaching aid and initiated an outdoor education program. It was not considered a replacement for classroom teaching but rather an additional aid—just as libraries, audiovisual materials, and language laboratories are important adjuncts to modern education. Bob Copland led its development with volunteer assistance from Jane Taylor, a community parent, before conceptualizing the children's garden idea. They created a "Teachers Manual" with the premise that all knowledge is interrelated, with some taught better in a classroom and some better outdoors. The manual was intended to make teaching outdoors easier and more meaningful for students and teachers. Educational activities included school camping and summer day camp programs focusing on pioneer life study along with constructing individual site improvement projects. This is when the log cabin was built in the Woods with community assistance including kids—Beth Hagenbuch and Lori Garver helped nail down the shingles. A rustic trail was constructed to provide access partially around the lake, a floating dock provided access to the water, and a footbridge allowed passage over Tihart Drain.

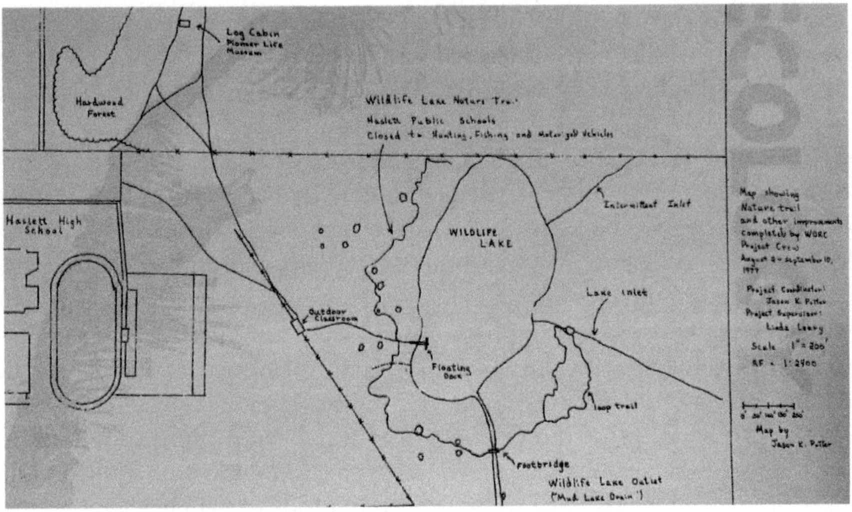

Figure 16.2. Wildlife Lake Educational Features Plan.
Image Credit: Haslett Public Schools

Earl Hatinger, a high school biology teacher, conducted water quality sampling with his class, finding dissolved oxygen levels at zero near the lake bottom and very few benthic organisms in the underlying muck. This condition indicated the eutrophication process to be well on its way. However, no further study was carried out to determine how quickly the process was going.

In recent years, middle school students have made use of the lake more frequently than high school groups. Bridget Booth, an eighth-grade science teacher and Conservation Club advisor at the middle school, envisions significant upgrades for the outdoor education program that draw from a "place-based education" concept. This idea immerses students into their local heritage, culture, landscape, and experiences with the natural world as a foundation for the study of language arts, math, social studies, science, and other subjects across the curriculum. So, in addition to creating a single nature study class elective, place-based educational content would be woven into other classes where appropriate, emphasizing how understanding our natural environment is fundamental to survival in a world that is quickly changing.

Wildlife Lake and its surroundings offer an outstanding laboratory for conducting these activities. Needed physical improvement projects like renovations to the trail and dock could be conducted by students and/or the community. Important hands-on educational activities would include biological assessments related to the health of the entire watershed. Water quality monitoring, birding, invasive species investigations, bug hunts, fish monitoring, and frog and toad surveys are all under consideration. Amphibians, in particular, are sensitive indicators of habitat quality, and their presence or absence can be used to assess wetland health. Learning to identify wetlands and understand the difference between wetland communities, such as bogs, marshes, fens, and wet-mesic flatwoods, would be important as well. Mud Lake's enchanting character continues to attract and impact kids and their parents in this time of increasing concern about climate change and the looming concern about dwindling biodiversity.

Getting Serious About Climate Change

Scientists are telling us global warming is happening, and no matter what is done, we are beyond the point of stopping it. Our only hope is to get resilient and adapt to it. Many folks comfortably rationalize how our species has successfully adapted to climate changes in the past, and however difficult it may be, we will figure it out. This is calming and could be true. Then again, the "acceleration" factor needs consideration. This is that curve with a radius that keeps getting shorter over time until things get wildly out of control or beyond adaptation capabilities. Acceleration typically shows up toward the end of a natural change process as exemplified by eutrophication of glacial lake basins and transitioning from one climate type to the next.

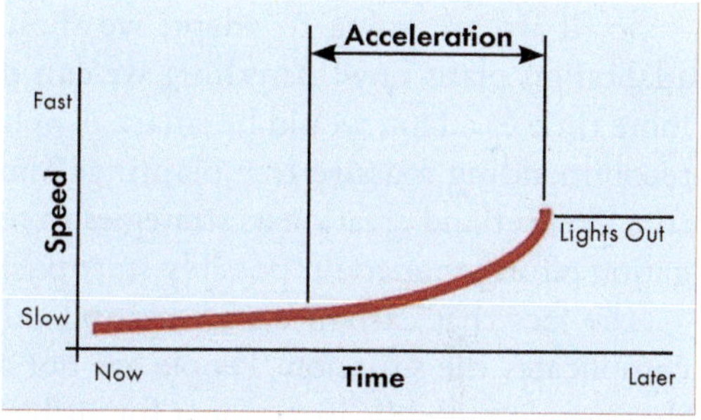

Figure 16.3. Acceleration is the process of gaining speed at an increasing rate overtime.

We are now seeing the effects of climate change in greater frequency than ever before, and warnings from climate experts say we can expect disastrous events to become increasingly worse. The summer of 2023 continued an upward spiral of record-breaking, climate-related events. Phoenix, Arizona, experienced the hottest July ever recorded by a U.S. city with a 31-day streak of highs at or above 110 °F and 3 days hitting 119 °F. Canada reported their worst-on-record wildfire season, causing inferior air quality across the continent along with mass evacuations from Yellowknife, in the Northwest Territories, and Kelowna, British Columbia. Deadly forest fires continued worldwide as a recurring nightmare. More than 65,000 hectares caught fire in Spain during the first half of 2023, representing 55% of burned land in the European Union. An August wildfire on Maui, in the Hawaiian Islands, killed more than 100 people, left nearly 1,000 unaccounted for, and burned around 2,200 structures—the deadliest U.S. fire in over a century. Seawater around coral reefs near the Florida Keys experienced record hot temperatures, triggering widespread coral bleaching indicating the entire ecosystem is under severe stress. This global pattern involving coral reefs is truly alarming since they support nearly 25% of all marine life. In late August, the first tropical storm hit Southern California since 1939 causing catastrophic flash flooding, damaging winds, and massive mud slides. And according to a report from the World Meteorological Organization, weather-related disasters resulting from climate change began breaking down any hope for normalcy in the South-West Pacific Ocean. The rise of sea level surrounding low-lying islands has threatened societal instability, and increasing ocean temperatures are imposing relentless harm to vulnerable marine ecosystems.

So, if we are going to adapt, we should be making and implementing adaptation plans now! Anything we can do to slow things down, giving us more time to adapt, would be smart as well. Many environmental experts are recommending massive tree plantings and other forms of green infrastructure like wetland creation as strategies to reestablish lost carbon sinks—mitigation efforts that could possibly start pushing the brake pedal.

The fact that carbon emissions and other greenhouse gases are invisible complicates the situation. People are not accustomed to fighting a problem they can't see. Public investment for visible change is much easier to sell. This explains why the Florida coastline is now lined with man-made infrastructure primarily created to attract snowbirds from northern states to empty their wealth into Florida's economy rather than to benefit manatees and other aquatic wildlife.

Manatees are large aquatic mammals, closely related to elephants, inhabiting Florida's coastal waters and feeding on underwater vegetation like seagrass. Florida manatees are listed as "threatened" under the federal Endangered Species Act of 1973 and are protected by law dating back to 1972. It is illegal to feed, harass, harm, pursue, hunt, shoot, wound, kill, annoy, or molest manatees. But it has apparently been okay to destroy their habitat—where they live. Finally, after years of haggling and a settlement reached between several nonprofit groups and the U.S. Fish and Wildlife Service, it was announced in June 2022 that the Service will update its manatee critical habitat protection requirements for the first time since 1976. With the noticeable disappearance of this species over the past decade, people are finally taking action.

Unfortunately, Florida's west coast was pummeled during Hurricane Ian's visit in late September 2022—another example of more frequent and intense storm activity associated with climate change—which caused severe ecosystem damage far beyond disturbances to remaining manatee habitat. Millions of insects and plants, and tens to hundreds of thousands of birds and animals were suddenly displaced, injured, and without food. Pollinators like bees, bats, butterflies, and the like saw all the pollen and nectar get blown into Georgia or the ocean. Surviving birds looking for insects found their food source decimated. Aside from direct hits on wildlife, windblown organic debris spilled into waterways, causing well-above-average nutrient loads, and chemicals stored in garages such as paint products, insecticides, fertilizers, and fuels were spewed over the landscape. While hurricanes may not appear as destructive as forest fires, the consequences are similar, resulting in environmental damage lasting for years.

Terry Sack, our greater Mud Lake area native, retired in Sarasota, Florida, roughly 60 miles north of Sanibel Island and Naples, which experienced the worst of Ian's rath. With maximum sustained winds of 150 miles per hour, it was the strongest storm to hit Florida since Hurricane Michael devastated the state in 2018. Terry and his neighbors live north of the storm's most destructive path, yet they were without power for more than five days. Homes in southern Sarasota County incurred over $33 million in damage with about 1,600 impacted structures and nearly 40 totally destroyed. From Florida's west coast to the Carolinas, a preliminary "best estimate" suggests the cost of overall damages totaled $67 billion—the costliest storm in Florida history.

Infrastructure recovery stories showed amazing effort by locals and volunteer workers from around the country. The bridge to Sanibel Island, which had several parts of its causeway ripped out, was repaired in only 15 days. After initially restoring power to more than two million customers in the first week following the storm, work continued into early October to repair outages for more than 70,000 people in the hardest hit areas. Private-property damage was another story. With many homeowners lacking adequate insurance, they needed to rely on family and friends to regain shelter.

Some of Terry's friends—the Oakley family—were among scores of Florida residents who lost their homes to Hurricane Ian. Fortunately, the Oakleys can rebuild with funding generated from a concert organized by Terry and his pals. These friends included the extended Allman Brothers Band family. Oteil Burbridge, part of the band family, hosted the concert at Crazy Uncle Mike's in Boca Raton, Florida. They billed it as the "Benefit for Berry Jr." and played Allman Brothers Band songs from 1971, '72, and '73.

Figure 16.4. Allman Brothers Band and Grateful Dead South Florida Family perform in a fundraising concert for Berry Duane Oakley and his family to rebuild their home.
Image credit: Phillip Nawroth

Burbridge, a longtime Allman Brothers Band member and current Dead & Company bassist, noted in a social media post: "Thanks to our Allman Brothers Band and Grateful Dead south Florida family for showing up Sunday night to support Berry Duane Oakley and his family. Your generosity was very touching, and we want to make sure you know how grateful we are for helping us raise $14,000 for Berry!" "Berry is a crucial part of the living legacy of the Allman Brothers Band," said Burbridge. "Let's show him and his family that they are not fighting this battle alone!"

Berry Jr., the son of late Allman Brothers Band bassist Berry Oakley, responded:

> We are OK. A bit frazzled but staying strong for each other. We are upside down and a mess trying to plan and find a new place to live while trying to keep each other's spirits up and the little kids happy and busy. We will be temporarily living in a hotel as we have four kids and a cat. When schools open, we'd love the kids to get back in school and have some kind of normalcy. We will have to work very hard to salvage whatever we can out of the house before it's condemned.

Unfortunately, the loss and damage incurred by people associated with climate change is disproportionate to that received by people who caused the problem. Certainly, Berry Oakley had very little to do with carbon emissions flooding our atmosphere for the past two centuries, but he and his family are paying dearly to adapt. On a global scale, this inequality is even more apparent. Many of the world's most climate-vulnerable countries are experiencing the brunt of climate-related disasters, even though they contributed little to instigating climate change. With most having few resources to adapt, they are looking for wealthier nations (the problem makers) to pay for damages.

Pakistan represents one example where extreme rainfall following a glacier-melting heat wave flooded nearly one-third of the country in the summer of 2022. Pakistan's farm fields turned into lakes, stranding communities for weeks. More than four million acres of productive farms including livestock were inundated. Over 1,700 people died, and millions lost their homes and livelihoods. A surge in malaria cases came next as mosquitoes bred in the stagnant water.

The outlook for nations bordering the equator looks considerably worse than here in the United States, but scientists are predicting water could rise more than three feet along our coastlines by 2100—a whopping 80 years or less from now—not very long! So, does it make sense to rebuild damaged coastal areas when the expectation is more damage in the near future? Given how much carbon dioxide (CO_2) is already in the air, a sea-level rise of seven more feet may be seen over the next 200 years. This seems far off, but it's only a few lifetimes—just a quick blip in the big picture. And before the oceans get that high, rising coastal groundwater levels will be destroying infrastructure, seeping into toxic storage areas, and opening sources for pollution to spill into our drinking water and coastal habitats long before our cities are inundated. Adaptation to a mess like this needs strategic thinking and quick action.

If our coasts become uninhabitable, where will people, buildings, water treatment plants, and transportation infrastructure move to? Our coasts are densely populated. Fifty percent of the U.S. population lives in coastal counties, and interior lands are predicted to become drier with limited desirable real estate. Forced migration away from the coasts could lead to serious conflicts over livable space and basic resources like food and freshwater.

One solution under consideration involves fortifying our coasts so that people and their infrastructure can stay in place. However, 20th century technology is not a reliable reference for how this should be done. In 2019, the Detroit River rose above the 100-year flood to the highest level in recorded history, representative of high water within all the Great Lakes at that time. Dropping slowly, this high-water condition lingered for almost two years. Homes, roads, parking lots, and hiking paths washed into the Great Lakes. Detroit witnessed neighborhood flooding and a seawall collapse separating a known contaminated site from the Detroit River. With extensive monitoring by the Michigan Department of Environment, Great Lakes, and Energy, no toxic spill was found—that time. However, following heavy spring rainstorms in 2023, visible signs of contamination showed up at the former McLouth steel mill site, farther south on the Detroit River, along the

Trenton Channel. Calcium hydroxide (or caustic lime), a substance similar to undiluted bleach that can cause chemical burns, appeared on the ground surface in cloudy white pools. Dead fish in the nearby Huntington Creek leading to the Trenton Channel indicated some of the toxic material is likely moving by way of groundwater.

Detroit is not alone in having contaminated sites next to the water. Seacoast regions are loaded with hazardous sites including military bases, chemical plants, landfills, and petroleum refineries. Older contaminated sites may be filled over or capped but are typically not protected against groundwater flooding. Toxins can move in unexpected directions when subjected to groundwater, as Michigan residents have seen with per- and polyfluoroalkyl (PFAS) contamination.

So, how do we protect ourselves from the legacy of our dirty past as water continues to rise? Moving forward on cleanup efforts that have been talked about for decades is a first step. Although expensive, this means digging out contaminated soils and chemically neutralizing them or moving them to a landfill on higher ground. Where necessary, the contaminants might require encasement in waterproof vaults. Excavated areas can be repurposed

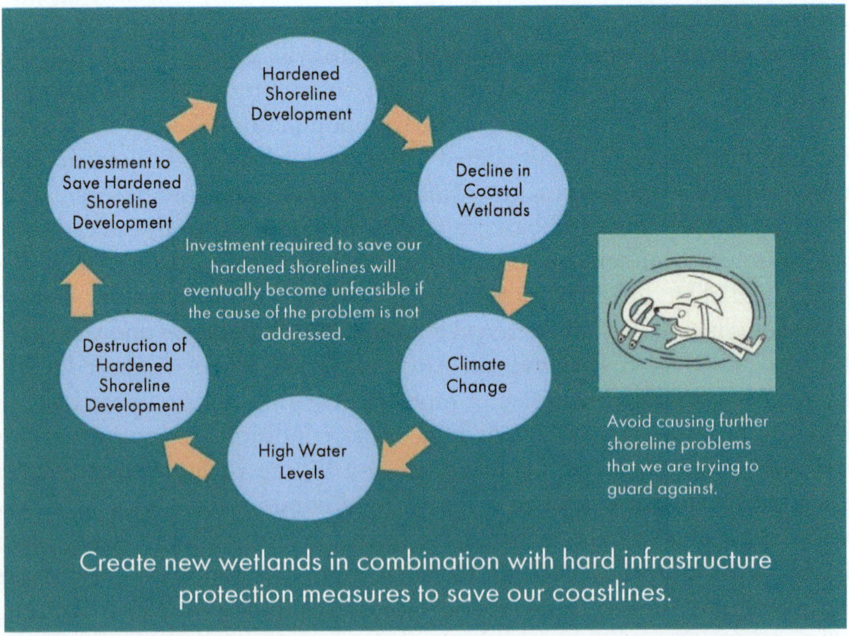

Figure 16.5. Diagram showing how hardening our coastlines without restoring wetlands will only cause further problems.

into newly created wetlands, which, in many cases, would restore what had been there in the past. More wetlands along with other variations of green infrastructure, like massive tree plantings, will be needed where the sea and groundwater are rising, along flood-prone inland rivers, and our Great Lakes shorelines. A solution that further hardens our shorelines without wetland and other green infrastructure creation will worsen the problem and send us on a circular path that can only end badly.

Wetlands take on many forms, but they typically are transitional areas between land and water, and they support a richly diverse web of plants and animals interacting together. How they receive water is the defining characteristic distinguishing two primary wetland types. Inland wetlands such as marshes (like that around Mud Lake) receive surrounding runoff from rivers and creeks, groundwater, and precipitation. Coastal wetlands do the same but are constantly affected by changing Great Lakes or seawater levels as well. Both inland and coastal wetlands provide the world with environmental cleansers along with food and water resources for many forms of life.

Coastal wetlands provide the added benefit of reducing storm surge impact and protecting land lying further inland—but not without a price. Intense storms with heavy rains and high winds can damage wetlands, filling them with debris and breaking them apart. In addition to intense storms, rising sea and Great Lakes water levels can damage coastal wetlands. Surveys show coastal wetlands in the eastern part of the United States are disappearing twice as fast as they can restore themselves. Based on National Aeronautics and Space Administration (NASA) satellite observations, Louisiana has lost enough wetlands since the mid-1950s to cover the entire state of Rhode Island. Some of these wetlands were submerged by rising seas; others were disturbed by hurricanes and some by oil or gas infrastructure installations. But coastal and river engineering caused most of the losses. How coastal and riparian projects are implemented can have tremendous positive or negative effects on wetlands.

On our Great Lakes coastlines, prior to when climate change was noticed, periodic changes in water levels occurred without all the drama we see today. Records regarding water fluctuations go back to 1860 with reliable and comparable data since 1900. While the lakes may stay high or low for several years, they always return to normal before going high or low again. The random nature of these fluctuations can only be attributed to the volume of rainfall in years preceding a change.

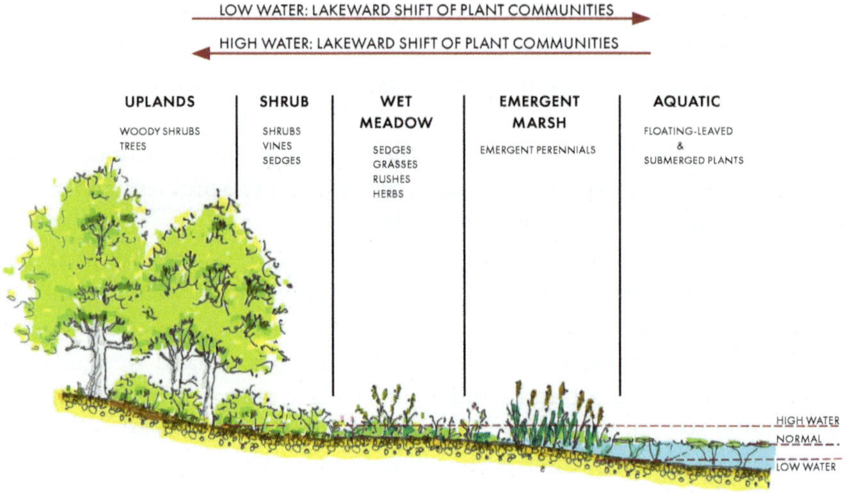

Figure 16.6. High water kills shrubs and causes them to move inland. Low water allows shrubs to advance lakeward. Gradual wetland decline and renewal enhances ecosystem vitality.

These fluctuations in water levels typically play out slowly over several years or decades and actually enhance coastal ecosystem vitality. High-water levels flood wetlands up to their high edge, stopping the spread of upland plants and allowing wetland plants to advance further inland. When filled with water, wetlands trap decaying plant fragments in the shallows, providing a niche for floating-leaved submergent plants like water lilies that enhance habitat for young fish, insects, and birds. When lake levels fall and stay low for several years, shrubs and trees take advantage of the dry soil and begin moving toward the shore. Cattails and bulrushes find themselves high and dry and can't withstand dehydration, so they also advance lakeward. Once reestablished offshore, they continue trapping sediment and organic debris. This dynamic process of gradual change enhances habitats and helps maintain Great Lake fishery productivity. Without this gradual change, the "wet meadow" zone, which is rich with pollinator attractions and habitat diversity, would not exist. Understanding this natural process can help in planning locations for new wetlands and can justify potential damage if it occurs soon after a wetland is created or restored. Water-level change is a natural and beneficial occurrence of destruction and renewal, but it can be alarmingly exaggerated and devastating when caused by climate change.

Even though wetland creation is a great solution to help protect our shorelines, it is not the silver bullet for climate change mitigation. Our only hope will require at least two large-scale actions having many variants for implementation.

- *Cutting back on carbon emissions.* Most importantly, cutting back on carbon emissions needs to happen. Scientists tell us that stabilizing earth's temperature requires a reduction of greenhouse gas emissions, down to net zero by 2050. This doesn't mean CO_2 emissions need to be at zero. They just need to be low enough to balance with CO_2 removed from the atmosphere, so that airborne CO_2 is no longer increasing—like in the old days before the Industrial Revolution. Rather than waiting until 2049 to begin reducing our emissions, it makes sense to do this gradually. So, a 45% reduction of global CO_2 emissions, from 2010 levels by 2030, is an established incremental target. Unfortunately, we aren't making any progress. Although the "rate" of carbon emission increase has slowed compared to before 2010, data showed global CO_2 emissions still increasing by an average of 1.4 global tonnes per year between 2011 and 2019. In 2020, a significant emission reduction of 5.4% occurred resulting from the world's inactivity during the COVID pandemic, but a rebound in 2021 was bigger than expected. So, overall, the change in CO_2 emissions over the past decade was essentially flat.

  Global CO_2 emissions primarily result from fossil fuel—the combustion of coal, oil, and natural gas. Coal is responsible for the bulk of it, representing approximately 41% of global fossil CO_2 emissions. Oil is the second largest contributor at 32%, with natural gas adding 21%. Other significant emissions come from industry like cement manufacturing. Of large contributing nations, China and India lead the rapid rise in fossil CO_2 emissions following the pandemic—already surpassing their pre-2019 record highs.

  The total global population emits about 34 billion tonnes of CO_2 each year, with the United States joining China and India as world leaders in this group. As the two most populated countries, China and India are both significant emitters of CO_2. China is in first place with 27% of the total. However, measuring total emissions doesn't present the whole story. For example, even though China is the highest emitter, the average American produces 14.4 tonnes of CO_2 per person compared to 7.1 tonnes for a Chinese person. So, in the most emissions per capita contest, the Americas become leaders over Asia and Oceania.

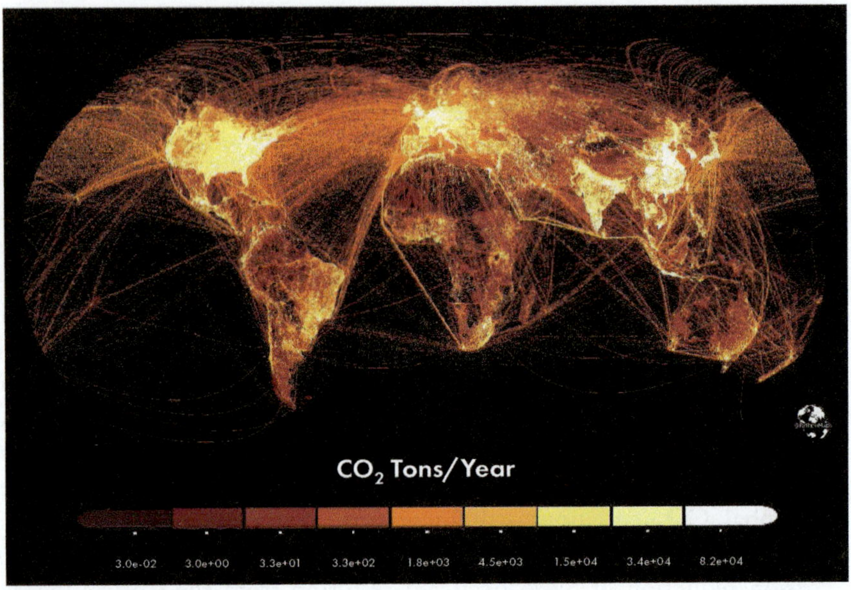

Figure 16.7. This map shows the world's CO_2 emissions and tonnes of CO_2 within 0.1x0.1 degree grid tiles in 2018.
Image Credit: PythonMaps

Population centers, flight paths, shipping lanes, and high-production areas are the primary fossil fuel users dispersing CO_2. Rethinking how all these systems work together using renewable energy is necessary to significantly reduce worldwide carbon emissions.

- *CO_2 removal.* A second large action involves removal of CO_2 from the atmosphere. There are both nature-based and technology-based approaches to accomplish this.

  Green infrastructure is the nature-based route, which includes mass planting of trees and prairies along with wetland, bioswale, and rain garden creation. In addition to slowing overland rain runoff to reduce flooding, all these measures can help restore the land as a natural carbon sink. Similar to how wetlands store carbon in the biomass of their plants, forests and prairies act the same way. Imagine how the Michigan mitten looked prior to its deforestation between 1850 and 1910—the "logging era" that got underway as European settlers gained control of the land. About 95% of the state was forested prior to this time. Likewise, much of the Midwest was covered with tallgrass prairie composed of plants extending their root systems as much as 12 feet deep—unlike corn, soybeans, sugar beets, and lawn that might go a foot below the surface at most. Losing these natural systems attributed to the loss of our carbon sequestration and storage areas. Reestablishing some of these areas will take decades and must begin now.

Technology-based approaches involve mechanical methods to remove CO_2 from the air. New cutting-edge facilities use giant fans to pull CO_2 out of the atmosphere and either store it underground in geological formations or reuse it (e.g., in synthetic fuel or in concrete). A facility in Iceland, known as Orca, operated by a company called Climeworks, captures 4,000 tonnes of carbon annually, pumping it underground where, when mixed with water, the gas cools and turns into stone. With 19 carbon-extraction facilities operating around the world, the International Energy Agency states that an average of 32 large-scale plants need to be built annually between now and 2050 to reach global climate goals.

All these strategies have drawbacks. Green infrastructure can be slow in maturing to a point where the plantings can effectively absorb carbon, and external threats like wildfires can quickly release years of carbon sequestration by forests. This is why green infrastructure strategies often involve ways to stop deforestation, restore cleared areas, and enable damaged woods to recover in addition to simply planting trees. Strategic placement of green infrastructure is important to maximize benefits as well. Buffering our lakes and rivers with wide swaths of green infrastructure will help to protect these water bodies from contaminants—phosphorus in particular, which accelerates the eutrophication process by optimizing conditions for algae growth. The western Lake Erie Basin, Saginaw Bay in Lake Huron, and Green Bay in Lake Michigan have all received dangerous levels of phosphorus from inland rivers passing through extensive farmlands and show severe degradation for it.

While carbon-removal facilities are considered critical to meeting international climate change targets, technologies to implement these facilities on a massive scale are not yet fully developed. Facilities built so far are removing only a tiny fraction of the CO_2 necessary to make a difference. Regardless, knowing a multi-pronged approach is required, the United States and United Kingdom are offering huge monetary incentives to groups developing direct air capture and related technologies.

Cutting back on carbon emissions is certainly the most effective strategy. However, transitioning our dependence on fossil fuel to renewable energy sources has not progressed far and is now, unfortunately, a political hot potato—even with the welfare of our next generation at stake. Yikes!

The Trump presidency stifled progress toward reducing CO_2 emissions in the United States in the past decade and unfortunately proclaimed the entire idea of climate change as a "non-issue" within his political agenda. So now, based on this misinformation and setback along with worldwide current trends, the challenge of reaching net-zero emissions by 2050 looks bleak. As American writer and novelist Kurt Vonnegut Jr. is often credited for saying (though proper attribution goes to environmental scientist Donella H. Meadows), "We'll go down in history as the first society that wouldn't save itself because it wasn't cost-effective."

Regardless, it makes no sense to do nothing about this ominous problem. In 2015 based on consensus among climate scientists, nearly every country in the world signed onto the Paris Agreement, a landmark international treaty pledging to limit the average global temperature increase to 1.5°C above pre-industrial levels. This represents a huge challenge given the planet's average temperature has already risen over 1°C, which is contributing to extinctions, lower crop yields, and more frequent wildfires. Unfortunately, the world is projected to exceed the 1.5°C threshold in the next four years. This breach may not be too serious if it is temporary and can be reduced in following years. But for that to happen, significant cultural changes need to be made on a global scale.

In a stark warning, the United Nations Environment Programme in 2022 reported incremental change is "no longer an option" and that avoiding dangerous levels of warming will require a "wide-ranging, large-scale, rapid and systemic transformation." The report finds that the world is likely heading for a warming of around a 2.6°C above pre-industrial levels under 2022 policies, though uncertainties in the climate system suggest that warming of up to 4°C cannot be ruled out. While some nations are making progress in adopting climate policies and accelerating clean energy deployment, there is a rapidly closing window to implementing adequate measures in time to put the world on track toward limiting global warming.

Climate change solutions involving long-standing mysteries about our oceans are under investigation, but the depth of new knowledge required to launch an ocean-based strategy is immense. Some things we know are helpful but are somewhat scary, like how seagrass meadows store globally significant amounts of carbon. This is great, but the bad news is these meadows have been degraded by worldwide coastal development, releasing tons of CO_2 into the atmosphere. Can restoration of these meadows be part of a multipronged approach?

We also know ocean water acts as the world's second largest carbon sink, absorbing at least one-quarter of the carbon emissions released into the atmosphere by human activity. As atmospheric CO_2 levels increase, more CO_2 dissolves into the ocean, increasing its CO_2 level as well. This helps to capture carbon, but when CO_2 is absorbed by seawater, chemical reactions occur causing the seawater to become more acidic. Excessive acidification threatens the chemical balance of ocean and coastal waters across the globe. This creates conditions that eat away minerals used by oysters, clams, shrimp, coral reefs, and other marine life to build their shells and skeletons. Human health is also a concern, as many harmful algal species produce more toxins and bloom faster in acidified waters.

In addition to CO_2 dissolving into the ocean's surface, it is pulled to the ocean depths by vertically rotating currents. Known as the Atlantic Meridional Overturning Circulation (AMOC), this large circular movement is caused by water cooling in the North Atlantic Ocean, near Greenland, causing it to become more dense and sink. It then pulls water from behind into the cooling position, which again sinks, pushing the water ahead down and back toward the south along the ocean floor—so goes this big circular movement in conveyor-belt fashion.

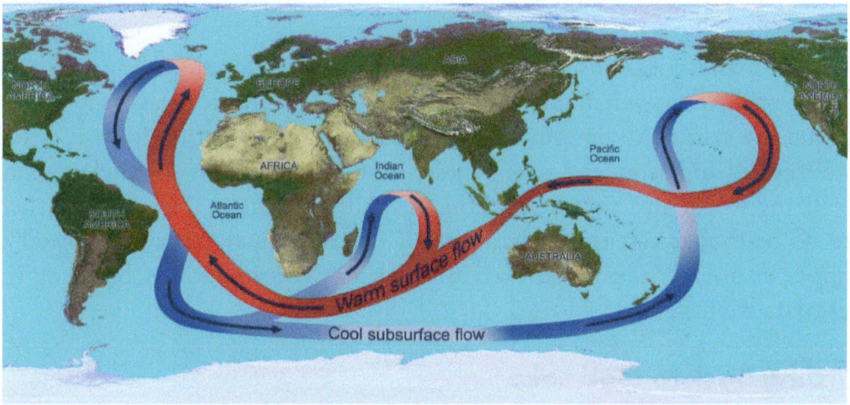

Figure 16.8. Illustration depicting the overturning circulation of the global ocean. Throughout the Atlantic Ocean, the circulation carries warm waters (red arrows) northward near the surface and cold deep waters (blue arrows) southward.
Image credit: NASA

The AMOC flushes much of the ocean floor with oxygenated water and other nutrients that support deep Atlantic ecosystems and moves larvae of marine organisms between different ocean regions. By sending dissolved CO_2 on the ocean surface to a deeper level, it increases the ocean's ability to absorb and store carbon. Most importantly for people, it redistributes warm water that builds up in the tropics, sharing the heat with northern areas. As warm water flows northward on the Atlantic Ocean surface, prevailing westerly breezes capture some of the warmth and carry it over Europe. This explains why western Europe is notably warmer than the eastern United States at the same latitude. However, scientists have observed a weakening of Atlantic circulation over the past 150 years, which is likely caused by climate change, and are concerned that this trend will continue. With ocean temperatures on the rise, fresh meltwater from Greenland could be diluting the salinity of water in the area where water-sinking takes place as part of the AMOC process. This reduced salinity results in the cold water becoming less dense, so it is not heavy enough to make a forceful plunge, thus slowing the conveyor belt. Although not expected to happen anytime soon, the collapse of the AMOC would wreak large-scale environmental disasters beyond the extinction of deepwater marine life. Other associated catastrophes could include rapid sea-level rise on the eastern coast of North America, significant cooling over Europe that disrupts agriculture, a parched Amazon rain forest, and disruption of Asian monsoons. Like other natural changes, the AMOC appears to have a well-established tipping point, and some evidence suggests this might come sooner than expected.

With many questions about the relationship of climate change and our oceans still unanswered, more monitoring and scientific analysis of ocean carbon are critical to determine if increased CO_2 absorption is wise. Effective stewardship strategies using these important data are equally essential. Realizing we are just now embarking on "climate change science," and there are no textbooks out there giving us all the right answers, actions need to happen as quickly as possible with all due safety considerations, based on the best data we have.

Circling Back to Mud Lake

Based on all the potential ways to mitigate climate change, reaching the established goal of net-zero carbon emissions by 2050 is not likely. So, with or without a plan, when tipping points are reached—triggering survival mode—people will quickly begin implementing their personal adaptation strategies. Folks are already beginning to seek refuge from rising sea levels, intensified hurricanes, relentless forest fires, and suffocating heat waves. And Michigan appears to be one of the most attractive destinations—especially for seacoast transplants. With the state's land safely averaging 900 feet above sea level and having 20% of the world's freshwater bordering its rich string of scenic shoreline destinations, what's not to like about Michigan? Think about all the places like historic Belle Isle, Mackinaw Island, Pictured Rocks, Tunnel of Trees, Sleeping Bear Dunes, Old Mission Peninsula, Keweenaw Peninsula, Tawas Point, Turnip Rock, Whitefish Point, and the list goes on—not to mention all the enchanting shoreline towns and gorgeous state parks. Porcupine Mountains Wilderness State Park is ranked the number one most beautiful state park in the United States. Its attractions include a 35,000-acre old growth forest; waterfalls, rivers, and streams; unrivaled vistas of the Lake Superior shoreline; and more than 90 miles of hiking trails. With thousands of miles of hiking and biking trails throughout the state, connecting all these beautiful places, Michigan is considered the number one trail state in the nation. The Detroit Riverwalk alone was named the "Best Riverwalk in America" by *USA Today* three years in a row!

Having great trails has become one of the defining metrics for quality places to live. Based on their friendly walking surface and minimally invasive footprint, they provide easy avenues for people to engage with nature, among other health-related benefits. So, it is no surprise that Michigan's trail system was largely advanced by people living near the network of wetlands surrounding Mud Lake! Nancy Krupiarz served as the first executive director for the Michigan Trails and Greenways Alliance, fostering and facilitating the creation of an interconnected statewide trails and greenways system while living north of Haslett Road, steps away from a wetland containing Mud Lake Drain (the inlet to Mud Lake). And Tom Woiwode, living south of Tihart Road next to another arm of the Mud Lake wetland, developed the GreenWays Initiative for the Community Foundation for Southeast Michigan. Through $33 million in foundation and private contributions and another $125 million of matching investments from government and other sources, the GreenWays Initiative helped more than 80 municipalities plan, design, finance, and build over 100 miles of connected trails across southeast Michigan.

Closer to home, Tom served Meridian Township as chairman of their Land Preservation Advisory Board. This group makes recommendations to the Township Board regarding property acquisitions for their Land Preservation Program and oversees stewardship planning for each property. The program was established in 2000 to acquire, preserve, and protect natural areas throughout the township having unique or special natural features.

Meridian Township officials have progressed immensely in their understanding about wetlands since the 1960s and steered clear of partisan pitfalls in promoting wetland importance. Their Land Preservation Program is a shining example of this effort. According to their Land Preserves web page, "The gift of permanence and the knowledge of these features will always be available for current and future generations to visit, appreciate, and enjoy." With focus on one example, in 2010, the township acquired 120 acres (three parcels) making up the Lake Lansing North Preserve with financial help from a Michigan Natural Resources Trust Fund grant. Situated adjacent to Ingham County's Lake Lansing Park North, the property displays mixed deciduous upland and lowland forests along with forested wetlands.

By autumn 2022, the township acquired 956 acres of the area's most beautiful, scenic, and natural lands. The Tihart Preserve, acquired in 2018, comprising 90 acres, is among 23 "preserve" properties. It borders both sides of Mud Lake Drain for nearly 2,000 feet within the massive wetland area east of Cornell Road.

Stewardship and land management plans for each preserve are under development, outlining necessary activities to protect or restore each site. This effort and that of Haslett Public Schools are the first meaningful attempts to publicly embrace and nurture the benefits of Mud Lake and its adjacent wetland areas.

It has been said that "Michigan is a lot like Alaska, only closer," but by 2050, climate experts say Michigan will likely have the current climate of Tennessee. This means more people need to start sniffing the marsh gas, because there is plenty more work to do in preparation for the millions of people that will likely migrate to the mitten. The state will need more housing, commercial development, roads, schools, airports, hospitals, waste management facilities, and more—along with more trees and wetlands! This time around, all this work needs to be done using nature-based solutions, keeping in mind the state's natural resources are why so many people are choosing Michigan over places like Ohio. Careful consideration will be needed in providing more drinking water. Although existing aquifers and groundwater wells currently serve Michigan's population well, more study is needed to determine future groundwater needs and the potential effects of climate change on projected rainfall amounts that will recharge the aquifers.

Mud Lake's attraction to kids living in the township did not end in the 1970s. Its challenging surroundings continue to entice young adventure seekers well into the 21st century. A transplant from Michigan's east side, Luke and Nate's pal, Nick, is one of many who finds enjoyment in hiking through the marsh to the lakeshore. Nick's mother, Carol, took a serious interest in the boys' swamping expeditions. Her Detroit-area upbringing did not offer many opportunities for natural-area engagement, but when it happened, she recognized its importance. Trips to Belle Isle and fishing with her dad near Port Huron and on Lake St. Clair made wonderful lifelong impressions. Finding a home in a newer subdivision near Lake Lansing, just north of Pine Lake Outlet, allows Nick to discover these kinds of magical experiences with his buddies.

Once the boys were in high school, Mud Lake became the focus of their outdoor encounters, resulting in after-school excursions through the soggy marsh around the lake. There just had to be fish in there, but shore fishing was pointless due to the wide ring of shallow water circling the lake's perimeter, loaded with emergent vegetation. With more reconnaissance and some wishful thinking, they found an abandoned aluminum boat in the lakeside brush, but it had no oars or paddles. No problem. They crafted some paddles from a pair of old crutches, Styrofoam sheeting, and duct tape. The paddles not only worked, but they floated when accidentally dropped into the water!

Realizing the boys were up to something that might be over the edge, Carol tagged along on their next trip to the lake. After seeing the boat float without taking on water, she could check both the "Safety" box and the "Wow, this looks like fun" box. Her return trip home to scrub down her sneakers conjured up pleasant memories of adventures on Michigan's eastside rivers and lakes. Meanwhile, the trio of fishermen, equipped with rubber worms and frogs, found the descendants of L.J.'s largemouth bass. Their catch and release fishing trips continued in 2019 to find descendants of Sam's and Randy Budzynski's northern pikes as well.

Figure 16.9. Nick's Mud Lake Bass

In the final decades of the 20th century, Meridian Township experienced a minor growth explosion spawned by more housing development, which triggered more commercial businesses. The Woods east of Cornell Road now hosts one of these subdivision expansions; the Pines is home to a condominium development; and the Park Lake Road gravel pits are surrounded by private residences. In addition to the new high school building on Marsh Road, new housing and shopping areas have sprung up from Haslett to Okemos along this entire corridor. Yet the massive wetland surrounding Mud Lake continues to provide ecosystem services.

With Mud Lake rapidly eutrophicating and our world heating up, we could be in our final rinse/spin cycle, and it will be interesting to see how we come out. Hopefully, we are not headed for another bleaching and trip back through the ringer. We are learning the real meaning of LSMFT—*L*iving *S*piritually *M*aterializes *F*rom *T*ruth. Knowing the truth about global warming and the positive effects wetlands can have both on our spirits and to sequester carbon, it's time to focus on our climate crisis. With some effort, we can make this problem into nothing more than another hot summer dance ending with only minor inconveniences like steamy car windows.

Nature engagement programs and meaningful environmental education opportunities similar to those conducted and under development at Mud Lake are extremely valuable for kids, and unsupervised exploration kicks the experience up a notch. Unfortunately, lands that once provided these opportunities are becoming scarce. So, more than ever before, ensuring places like Mud Lake continue providing ecosystem services while rendering enjoyment for people long into the future is critical to our healthy survival.

References

In Hot Water: Ocean Heat and Our Warming World, Nat'l Oceanic & Atmospheric Admin. (Apr. 3, 2023), https://storymaps.arcgis.com/stories/51c41fd3f78c4939a28b016e0ddb5109.

The Ancient Pathways of African Elephants, Wayfairer, https://www.wayfairertravel.com/inspiration/ancient-pathways-of-african-elephants/ (last visited May 31, 2023).

Michael Bednar, *Humans Not the Only Ones Affected by Hurricane Ian*, Englewood Rev. (Nov. 4, 2022), https://englewoodreview.com/main.asp?SectionID=10&SubSectionID=427&ArticleID=8191&fbclid=IwAR2O79vUDRvyZEjm6a0V4Q4wmp7AW8lAKo5Ge3yN0drc297i3SVUZBXhdlI.

Leigh Beeson, *Monarch Butterfly Populations Are Thriving in North America*, UGA Today (June 10, 2022), https://news.uga.edu/monarch-butterfly-populations-are-thriving/.

Telephone Interviews and E-mail Correspondence With Bridget Booth, Certified Environmental Educator, Science Teacher at Haslett Middle School (Mar. 2 - Apr. 22, 2022).

Michael Carlowicz, *Watery Heatwave Cooks the Gulf of Maine*, NASA Earth Observatory (Aug. 8, 2018), https://earthobservatory.nasa.gov/images/92734/watery-heatwave-cooks-the-gulf-of-maine.

Jennifer Chu, *Explained: The 1.5 C Climate Benchmark*, MIT News, Aug. 27, 2023, https://news.mit.edu/2023/explained-climate-benchmark-rising-temperatures-0827.

Monica Echeverria, *Migratory Monarch Butterfly Now Classified as Endangered*, World Wildlife Fund (July 27, 2022), https://www.worldwildlife.org/stories/migratory-monarch-butterfly-now-classified-as-endangered.

European Commission CORDIS, *Atlantic Ocean Circulation Is Weakening; Are Our Deep-sea Ecosystems at Threat?*, https://cordis.europa.eu/article/id/123241-atlantic-ocean-circulation-is-weakening-are-our-deepsea-ecosystems-at-threat (last updated Apr. 13, 2018).

Paula Gardner, *Demands for Cleanup at Contaminated Michigan industrial site. 'Job is not done'*, Bridge Michigan (July 5, 2023), https://www.bridgemi.com/business-watch/demands-cleanup-contaminated-michigan-industrial-site-job-not-done

Goodreads, *Donella H. Meadows Quotable Quote*, https://www.goodreads.com/quotes/11432253-we-ll-go-down-in-history-as-the-first-society-that (last visited May 31, 2023) ("We'll go down in history as the first society that wouldn't save itself because it wasn't cost-effective.").

Carolyn Gramling, *The New UN Climate Change Report Shows There's No Time for Denial or Delay*, ScienceNews (Aug. 9, 2021), https://www.sciencenews.org/article/climate-change-un-ipcc-report-humans.

Telephone Interviews and E-mail Correspondence With Beth Hagenbuch, Landscape Architect (Feb. 11 - Apr. 5, 2022).

Rodney Hagenbuch, Rodney Hagenbuch Memoir (1965) (unpublished manuscript).

Zeke Hausfather, *Global CO_2 Emissions Have Been Flat for a Decade, New Data Reveals*, CarbonBrief (Nov. 4, 2021), https://www.carbonbrief.org/global-co2-emissions-have-been-flat-for-a-decade-new-data-reveals/.

Zeke Hausfather & Daisy Dunne, *UNEP: Meeting Global Climate Goals Now Requires "Rapid Transformation of Societies,"* CarbonBrief (Oct. 27, 2022), https://www.carbonbrief.org/unep-meeting-global-climate-goals-now-requires-rapid-transformation-of-societies/.

Kristina Hill, *The Big Idea: How Can We Adapt to Life With Rising Seas?*, Guardian (Feb. 21, 2022), https://www.theguardian.com/books/2022/feb/21/the-big-idea-how-can-we-adapt-to-life-with-rising-seas.

John Hiner, *Letter From the Editor: Get Ready, Michigan—Climate Migrants Will Be Seeking "a Pleasant Peninsula" in Droves*, MLive (Dec. 13, 2022), https://www.mlive.com/news/2022/12/letter-from-the-editor-get-ready-michigan-climate-migrants-will-be-seeking-a-pleasant-peninsula-in-droves.html.

Walter J. Hoagman, Great Lakes Wetlands: A Field Guide (1998).

Tasmiha Khan, *All the Ways to Remove Carbon Emissions From the Air*, Time (Oct. 27, 2022), https://time.com/6213489/remove-carbon-emissions-from-air/.

Kevin Lee, *Environmental Problems Associated With Coastal & Inland Wetlands*, Sciencing (Apr. 24, 2017), https://sciencing.com/environmental-problems-associated-coastal-inland-wetlands-23457.html.

Meridian Township, *Land Preserves*, https://www.meridian.mi.us/community/explore-meridian/land-preserves (last visited May 31, 2023).

Andrew O'Brien, *UPDATE: Benefit Concert Raises $14,000 for Berry Oakley Jr. & Family After Hurricane Ian Destroys Their Home [Photos]*, Live for Live Music (Oct. 18, 2022), https://liveforlivemusic.com/news/berry-duane-oakley-benefit-home-destroyed-hurricane-ian/.

Stefan Rahmstorf, *Is the Atlantic Overturning Circulation Approaching a Tipping Point?*, YouTube (Mar. 21, 2022), https://www.youtube.com/watch?v=4iJEcInbyn0.

Telephone Interviews and E-mail Correspondence With Terry Sack, Security, Promotion, and Support to Nationally Touring Musical Acts (Oct. 15 - Dec. 12, 2022).

Bethany Tietjen, *Loss and Damage: Who Is Responsible When Climate Change Harms the World's Poorest Countries?*, Conversation (Nov. 3, 2022), https://theconversation.com/loss-and-damage-who-is-responsible-when-climate-change-harms-the-worlds-poorest-countries-192070.

Sally Younger, *Satellites Help Scientists Track Dramatic Wetlands Loss in Louisiana*, NASA Jet Propulsion Lab'y (Nov. 7, 2022), https://www.jpl.nasa.gov/news/satellites-help-scientists-track-dramatic-wetlands-loss-in-louisiana.

Epilogue

World-wide climate change-related disasters continued throughout 2023. Flooding in Libya claimed over 5,000 deaths and thousands more are unaccounted for, due to a ferocious storm that first swept over Bulgaria, Greece, and Turkey, where it also caused flooding and killed more than 20 people. The storm transitioned into a "medicane" when it passed over the Mediterranean Sea, which is somewhat rare but has similar characteristics to hurricanes. Aging dams and missed warnings exacerbated the catastrophe, as huge walls of water poured down mountains toward Derna, a coastal Libyan city, wiping out entire neighborhoods.

As smoke from Canadian wildfires dissipated in the United States, the hurricane season ramped up. Idalia slammed into Florida's west coast in late August as a high-end category 3 hurricane with 125mph winds, flooding streets, snapping trees, ripping off roofs, and cutting power. With the speed of a fast-moving train, it quickly blew into Georgia and South Carolina, continuing to flood roadways and sending people in a scramble for higher ground. Initial damage cost estimates ranged from $9 billion to $20 billion—much less than Hurricane Ian, which tore up a more heavily populated area of Florida in 2022. However, an estimate for the cost of environmental damage where Idalia hit, known as Florida's "nature coast", was not available.

A beaver scampers along the Detroit River Walk near the carousel where figurines shaped as animals native to the area's historic ecosystem serve as riding seats.
Image credit: Detroit Riverfront Conservancy.

But there is good news too! Based on diligent efforts to preserve, restore, and recreate natural habitats like wetlands, forests, and prairies in Michigan, several animal species, previously considered endangered or nearly extinct, are on the comeback. Lake sturgeon are returning in large numbers to the Detroit and Saint Clair

Rivers. Beavers are showing up on the Detroit and Rouge Rivers. Bald eagles seem to be everywhere, along with monarch butterflies, and even black bear sightings are becoming common in the upper half of the mitten. Native predator fish are resurging in the Great Lakes, with the Lower Detroit River and Western Lake Erie Basin recognized as the walleye capital of the world. Water bodies regarded as dead in the 1960s are now teaming with life.

More importantly, the reality of climate change is starting to sink into the minds of many, and prudent actions are beginning—at least from a planning standpoint. "Climate action plans" generally include greenhouse gas emission reduction targets and detailed action steps to help meet their goals. The plans may include additional components such as resilience strategies and clean energy targets along with economic and social goals. Individual characteristics of local economy, resource base, and political structure provide differing opportunities for addressing climate change in various regions.

At the national level, the White House released an executive order in January 2021, during President Biden's first month in office, putting the climate crisis at the center of U.S. foreign policy and national security. Recognizing the United States and the world face a profound climate crisis, the order calls for a government-wide approach in creating or updating climate action plans. More than 20 federal agencies complied including:

1. Department of Agriculture
2. Department of Commerce
3. Department of Defense
4. Department of Education
5. Department of Energy
6. Department of Health and Human Services
7. Department of Homeland Security
8. Department of Housing and Urban Development
9. Department of the Interior
10. Department of Justice
11. Department of Labor
12. Department of State
13. Department of the Treasury
14. Department of Transportation
15. Department of Veterans Affairs
16. General Services Administration
17. National Aeronautics and Space Administration
18. Office of Personnel Management

19. Smithsonian Institution
20. U.S. Agency for International Development
21. U.S. Army Corps of Engineers
22. U.S. Environmental Protection Agency
23. U.S. International Development Finance Corporation

President Biden continued meeting with leaders of the Major Economies Forum on Energy and Climate (MEF) into 2023 to galvanize efforts needed to tackle the climate crisis and keep the established 1.5°C limit on global warming within reach. The administration is also assisting developing countries in taking stronger climate action, including providing support to the Green Climate Fund, the Amazon Fund, and other related activities. MEF leaders are looking at ways to accelerate four key areas necessary for limiting global warming to 1.5°C as well. These include:

- **Decarbonizing energy**: Announcing steps to drive down emissions in the power and transportation sectors, including scaling up of clean energy, setting ambitious 2030 zero-emission vehicle goals, and decarbonizing international shipping.
- **Ending deforestation of the Amazon and other critical forests**: Working through the Forest and Climate Leaders' Partnership to mobilize public, private, and philanthropic support.
- **Tackling potent, non-CO_2 climate pollutants**: Launching a Methane Finance Sprint to cut methane emissions and accelerating hydrofluorocarbon phasedown under the Kigali Amendment.
- **Advancing carbon management**: Partnering with countries to accelerate carbon capture, removal, use, and storage technologies through a COP 28 Carbon Management Challenge to deal with emissions that can't otherwise be avoided.

The great state of Michigan is among 33 others having their own climate action plan. The "MI Healthy Climate Plan" was developed by the Michigan Department of Environment, Great Lakes, and Energy (EGLE), with contributions from hundreds of Michiganders through thousands of hours of research, reflection, and conversation. It is available for everyone to see at Michigan.gov/EGLE.

The plan lays out a broad vision for fulfilling Gov. Gretchen Whitmer's commitment to achieve 100% economy-wide carbon neutrality by 2050—

the global, science-based benchmark for reducing greenhouse gas (GHG) emissions to avoid the most devastating and costly impacts of climate change. Sustained, aggressive action across Michigan's economy is necessary to reach desired targets. Summaries of key recommendations are provided below, which are fleshed out in detail within the plan.

Commit to Environmental Justice and Pursue a Just Transition: Ensure that at least 40 percent of state funding for climate-related and water infrastructure initiatives benefit Michigan's disadvantaged communities (in line with the federal government's Justice40 guidelines for federal funding); that Justice40 is developed in partnership with leaders in disadvantaged communities; and that Michigan emphasizes a just transition for all workers through proactive engagement, job training, and workforce development.

Clean the Electric Grid: Generate 60 percent of the state's electricity from renewable resources and phase out remaining coal-fired power plants by 2030. Limit energy burden from powering and heating homes to not more than 6 percent of annual income for low-income households.

Electrify Vehicles and Increase Public Transit: Build the infrastructure necessary to support 2 million electric vehicles on Michigan roads by 2030. Increase access to clean transportation options—including public transit—by 15 percent each year.

Repair and Decarbonize Homes and Businesses: Reduce emissions related to heating Michigan homes and businesses by 17 percent by 2030. Increase investments in repairing and improving buildings to reduce costs for working families and small businesses.

Drive Clean Innovation in Industry: Encourage clean innovation hubs where private enterprises strategically co-locate and collaborate to develop and deploy new, cleaner manufacturing technologies and conduct research and development to reduce emissions from hard to decarbonize industries. Triple Michigan's recycling rate to 45 percent and cut food waste in half by 2030.

Protect Michigan's Land and Water: Protect 30 percent of Michigan's land and water by 2030 to naturally capture GHG emissions, maintain and improve access to recreational opportunities for all Michiganders, and protect biodiversity. Leverage innovative strategies to support climate-smart agriculture.

Within the last section titled "Protect Michigan's Land and Water," the plan claims:

> Many of the state's powerful natural carbon sinks have been developed or converted and lost their natural ability to store carbon, increasing net GHG emissions. Wetlands, in particular, are important carbon sinks and stocks. Building out green waterway infrastructure, like constructed wetlands, can yield both climate adaptation and mitigation benefits. This Plan recommends

avoiding further land-use conversions that increase GHG emissions and stewarding Michigan's natural resources by implementing land-use strategies that reduce GHG emissions in partnership with Michigan's tribal governments.

In addition to addressing climate change issues close to home, these plans support the Paris Climate Accord and demonstrate commitments to achieving goals agreed upon by the international community to curb global warming and help rebuild the world's economies stronger, greener, and better. The Paris Agreement calls for the transformation of global production and consumption patterns into a "circular economy," in which excessive consumption, waste, and use of fossil fuels would be avoided by leasing, reusing, repairing, and recycling existing materials and products. The extraction and processing of natural resources causes half of global emissions and over 90% of biodiversity loss. Shifting to a circular economy is the path forward to achieving the Paris Climate Accord goal of limiting global temperature rise to 1.5° C above pre-industrial times.

Circular economy principles include using less resources and more sustainable materials along with recycling materials previously used. Energy supply, transportation, buildings, and waste management are priority sectors for immediate climate action. Implementation strategies outlined in the aforementioned plans will support the Paris Climate Accord agenda and move our

A photo from the "MI Healthy Climate Plan" emphasizing the importance of wetlands.
Photo credit: MI Dept. of Environment, Great Lakes, and Energy.

country toward a circular economy, while making our communities more sustainable, resilient, affordable, and better prepared to manage the impacts of climate change.

In September 2023, the White House announced funding to create the American Climate Corps. The program is designed to put more than 20,000 young people on career pathways in the growing fields of clean energy, conservation, and climate change. It will provide training for a wide range of actions including restoring coastal wetlands, managing forests to prevent fires, and implementing energy efficient solutions to reduce energy costs. The Corps will focus on equity and environmental justice—prioritizing communities traditionally left behind, including energy-based communities that powered our nation for generations. A coordinated recruitment process among several federal agencies will work with AmeriCorps, which will initiate a new "American Climate Corps hub" to support the program.

Michigan and nine other states are moving forward with Climate Corps programs as well. Funded through public-private partnerships, including AmeriCorps, some states are already demonstrating the power of skills-based training as a tool to expand pathways into good-paying jobs. The Michigan Healthy Climate Corps will engage 30 AmeriCorps participants to support the state in achieving economy-wide carbon neutrality by 2050. Developing a network of young leaders to assist communities on a professional level is underway to accelerate climate action.

And wouldn't you know, Meridian Township is among hundreds of municipalities with their own climate action plan, which mirrors other plans and addresses climate issues specifically related to their jurisdiction. In 2007, Meridian Township joined over 1,000 communities across the United States in signing the U.S. Mayors' Climate Protection Agreement. Ten years later, Meridian resolved to achieve the goals of the Paris Climate Accord and adopted a "Climate Sustainability Plan." Wetlands cover over 25% of Meridian Township, and its leaders are in complete understanding of how these areas play key roles in maintaining healthy watersheds and communities while providing resilience against extreme precipitation events. As such, water and green infrastructure management are called out as a high priorities within the plan, in addition to addressing energy efficiency, renewable energy, recycling and waste reduction, and transportation. A primary objective of the plan's focus on water and green infrastructure management is to protect wetland ecosystem health and services by strengthening policies and activities that favor wetland area expansion, enhance wetland quality and resilience, and expand efforts to assure public awareness of the value and stewardship of wetlands.

This kind of policymaking elevates the importance of Mud Lake even further. Let's face it, Mud Lake has been doing its job for over 10,000 years and will continue long into the future. But people may not be around to watch if we don't get with the new programs. It would be unimaginable if all the human well-being benefits from wetlands had no one to help; if there was no one to celebrate the return of monarch butterflies; if all the riches of herbs and spices just decayed into the soil; if nobody swatted at deer flies, carved their initials in trees, examined small things around woodland pond edges, caught fish through holes in the ice; or if kids weren't around to experience their shoes getting stuck in the mud.

This narrative showcases only a snippet of planning iniatives that are underway to combat climate change. Enough strategies are emerging to fill another book about revolutionizing agricultural practices. Eliminating the need for herbicides and pesticides in addition to producing higher, more nutritious yields are part of the exciting expectations. Some of the ideas involve "regenerating" our soil by adding carbon, which further builds our arsenal to mitigate climate change while helping to solve worldwide food shortage problems. Furthermore, funding incentives to make all these plans happen are coming out faster than people can grab onto, and millions more in funds are in the pipeline.

Circling back to "carbon neutrality," whereby carbon dioxide released into the atmosphere is balanced by an equivalent amount removed, is the only solution. How we get there will take multiple actions. Fortunately, the wheels on the climate action train are beginning to roll. National, state, and local plans and programs are springing up in a flurry. Becoming familiar with them is a first step. Realizing they reflect bipartisan ideology and, in fact, are roadmaps for human survival is easy to see after understanding how Earth is our life support system. Governing agencies are committed to these plans and typically welcome additional ideas for plan enhancements. However, these plans can only set policy. In the end, businesses, institutions, and individuals need to step up as implementers. As we make the next 20 or so cosmic journeys around the sun, Earth-sensitive actions, both large and small, taken by everyone, will determine the nature of our future.

References

CNN, *Aging dams and missed warnings: A lethal mix of factors caused Africa's deadliest flood disaster* (Sept. 15, 2023), https://www.cnn.com/2023/09/14/middleeast/lethal-factors-leading-to-libya-floods-intl/index.html.

Center for Climate and Energy Solutions, *U.S. State Climate Action Plans* (Dec. 2022), https://www.c2es.org/document/climate-action-plans/#:~:text=Author(s)&text=33%20states%20have%20released%20a,of%20revising%20or%20developing%20one.

Executive Order 14008, Tackling the Climate Crisis at Home and Abroad (Jan. 27, 2021), https://www.whitehouse.gov/briefing-room/presidential-actions/2021/01/27/executive-order-on-tackling-the-climate-crisis-at-home-and-abroad/.

White House, Fact Sheet: President Biden to Catalyze Global Climate Action through the Major Economies Forum on Energy and Climate (Apr. 20, 2023), https://www.whitehouse.gov/briefing-room/statements-releases/2023/04/20/fact-sheet-president-biden-to-catalyze-global-climate-action-through-the-major-economies-forum-on-energy-and-climate/#:~:text=President%20Biden%20has%20set%20an,by%20no%20later%20than%202050.

White House, Fact Sheet: Biden Administration Releases Agency Climate Adaptation and Resilience Plans from Across Federal Government (Oct. 7, 2021), https://www.whitehouse.gov/briefing-room/statements-releases/2021/10/07/fact-sheet-biden-administration-releases-agency-climate-adaptation-and-resilience-plans-from-across-federal-government/.

White House, Fact Sheet: Biden-Harris Administration Launches American Climate Corps to Train Young People in Clean Energy, Conservation, and Climate Resilience Skills, Create Good-Paying Jobs and Tackle the Climate Crisis (Sep 20, 2023), https://www.whitehouse.gov/briefing-room/statements-releases/2023/09/20/fact-sheet-biden-harris-administration-launches-american-climate-corps-to-train-young-people-in-clean-energy-conservation-and-climate-resilience-skills-create-good-paying-jobs-and-tackle-the-clima/.

Michigan Department of Environment, Great Lakes, and Energy, MI Healthy Climate Plan (Apr. 2022), https://www.michigan.gov/egle/-/media/Project/Websites/egle/Documents/Offices/OCE/MI-Healthy-Climate-Plan.pdf.

MI Healthy Climate Corps, *Announcing the MI Healthy Climate Corps* https://www.mihealthyclimatecorps.org/ (last visited Sep. 26, 2023).

Michigan Department of Environment, Great Lakes, and Energy, *EGLE announces MI Healthy Climate Corps to launch in January* (Aug .29, 2023), https://www.michigan.gov/egle/newsroom/mi-environment/2023/08/29/mi-healthy-climate-corp-to-launch-in-january#:~:text=The%20MI%20Healthy%20Climate%20Corps%20(MHCC)%20is%20a%20soon%2D,for%20progress%20toward%20a%20healthy%2C.

United Nations, Climate Change, *Shifting to a Circular Economy Essential to Achieving Paris Agreement Goals* (Apr 15, 2021), https://unfccc.int/news/shifting-to-a-circular-economy-essential-to-achieving-paris-agreement-goals.